Stalking &
Catching
Trout

Stalking & Catching Trout

Les Hill and
Graeme Marshall

Line drawings
by Grant Winter

The Halcyon Press

Published by
The Halcyon Press.
A division of
Halcyon Publishing Ltd.
P.O. Box 360, Auckland 1015, New Zealand.

Printed in China
by
Prolong Press Limited

ISBN 1-877256-57-9

Contents

Acknowledgements

Stalking and Catching Trout has been written whilst running a seven days a week business. My contribution has depended on the generosity of my wife, Raewyn, and our wonderful staff who have allowed me time out on a regular basis in order that our deadline could be met.

Graeme Marshall

I would like to thank the following people who appear in the photographs of this book. Each has made a contribution which is valued and appreciated. The names are listed in the order that they appear. Ho Hill, Len Cook, John Cornish, Frank Sullivan, Alan Pannett, Philip Sanford, Brian Smith, Eden Shields, John Taylor, Damon Smith, Bob Worley, Ross Taylor, Tim Varley and Tony Allen.

My brother Ho took the cover photograph and several others of me that appear. John Cornish also shot one. I thank them for their help and the lessons I learn from their photographic skills. Jack Taylor edited the whole manuscript for Graeme and I. His comments and alterations were invaluable. We thank Jack sincerely for his time and interest. John Cornish and Ho Hill also assisted me with my contribution to the text. Their comments provided fresh views about the content and added accuracy to the final copy. Thanks to them.

I am also grateful to Alistair Marshall who applied his computer skills in arranging and presenting the illustrations in Chapter 2.

Les Hill

Introduction

In 1985 *Stalking Trout* was first published. This was followed by *Catching Trout* in 1991. Each book has been reprinted several times and each has been remarkably popular and successful. While the content of both books is still quite relevant, Graeme and I believe there is much more to be told about the craft of hunting trout, much more to add to what we have already written. We also feel that the two books will blend easily and naturally into one volume — like an angler stalks a trout and then attempts to lure it on a river. Since 1985 Graeme and I have had many new angling experiences. Graeme has guided hundreds of anglers to thousands of fish in both the backcountry and close to his home during 1600 more fishing days. He has also managed to ensnare a few himself.

My streamside forays in the last twenty years have all been as a recreational angler. I have enjoyed about fifty days of fishing each year — another 1000 days more fun with several thousand trout brought to shore. If each trout caught offered a little lesson — and I believe it did — then much has been learned.

Stalking And Catching Trout is not just a revision of the original books — it is a complete rewrite. We have deliberately avoided revisiting the original texts frequently so that we could maintain a fresh focus. The book has been separated into two parts. Part One — Stalking Trout — has been written by me. It focuses specifically on finding trout. Greater emphasis has been placed on reading rivers, their beds, banks, vegetation and waters than there was in *Stalking Trout*. Some information about stalking still water margins has been included in Part One.

Part Two — Catching Trout — was Graeme's responsibility (except chapter 10 which I penned). It is essentially about catching trout which have been spotted, or high percentage blind fishing in promising waters as identified in the first half. It is our hope that we have produced a much more complete stalker's guide than we previously did.

The photographic content of *Stalking And Catching Trout* is all new and was part of my contribution. As anglers and readers of angling literature we understand how difficult it is to make photographs meaningful to all who view them. We have endeavoured to incorporate vivid visual images to enhance the text, as well as to convey some of the exhilaration and splendour we experience while out fishing.

The line drawings were again sketched by Grant Winter. Grant has stalked trout with both Graeme and me, so he not only produces visually pleasing images but also incorporates a clear understanding of his subject in each picture.

The Ultimate Stalk

I have always believed that to stalk and catch a trout is the ultimate fishing experience. It is an experience which one can seemingly never tire of. Every fish feeds in a different place, feeds in a different way, reacts individually. Every fish offers a unique challenge and new excitement. The pursuit of even a thirty-five centimetre trout can enormously excite and engross an angler for as long as it takes to bring it to shore.

However, if there is an experience which betters "the ultimate" it must be when a monstrous fish is discovered, pursued, fooled and finally laid on its side out of the water when its full grandeur can be appreciated. Last summer Brian Smith (Smithy) and I shared such an occasion. We were totally absorbed from the moment the fish slipped into view until it sprayed us with water as it sped back to freedom when released.

Trophy trout (four and a half kilograms or more) are not found in every river. However, those waterways that do hold them seem to harbour their share season after season. I'm not certain why some rivers are trophy nurturers and some are not but it must relate somehow to the availability and quality of the food supply and to the dynamics of the fish population. There is no doubt that the river configuration is important too. Really big fish like to be close to "big" (deep) water. They also occupy locations that contain a stable riverbed composed of large stones, boulders or solid bedrock. Smithy and I were aware of these desirable features. We were stalking up a "trophy river." That added a little excitement to every step we took upstream — added urgency to our pace over barren reaches or lifted us onto tiptoe along likely edges.

Really big trout are exceedingly wary. We knew this too. Along edges likely to hold fish, we were not only on tiptoe but eased upstream in a tense crouch, heads pushed forwards, necks extended — ready to "freeze" the instant any fish came into view. Smithy was right at my shoulder. We approached a bank which overhung a deep fast run — the sort of place where a big fish would hover right against the shore. "There has to be one here," ventured Smithy. Nervously we dropped to our knees and a stoop became a crawl. Heads down, bottoms raised somewhat, we peered down into the water. Only the top of our heads and eyes extended over the bank. Nothing. I swivelled my eyes upstream. Nothing. Then, in my peripheral vision, I caught a movement. The shape drifted out from under the bank, paused, then retreated. "Did you see that?" I whispered.

"I did. You see the size of it?" — the emphasis on "size."

"Did."

A short vigil began. Four eyes willing the fish to appear again, proof that it really existed, proof that it had not been alarmed. However, it remained out of sight. After several long minutes Smithy relented. "Have a closer look," he said. I shuffled forwards, craned my neck. The bank overhang was pronounced. I lifted my chin even more, peered over my nose. Two things came into view — the tip of a trout's snout, extending forwards from a lip in the bank, then an eye-popping distance downstream, the tip of a caudal fin waving in the flow. "He's still there," the whisper even quieter — softened by the obvious size of the fish.

I pulled back, concerned that if the fish moved out to a nymph in the faster water it would see me. There was no doubt that we had to tempt this fish. But how? Downstream, the water was two metres deep right to the shore. A thicket of matagouri atop the bank, prevented a bank-side cast. The only way to present a nymph was by dropping it suspended from the rod tip on about two metres of nylon. We'd used the technique to fish under overhangs many times. We knew the incredible excitement of watching a huge fish so close dive for a nymph.

"You watch and tell me when to strike," said Smithy. Obviously it was his turn! At least I'd witness the take. While Smithy attached a weighted nymph to his tippet I snaked forward on my stomach then cautiously and ever so slowly pushed my head out until I could see the snout once more. It hovered less than two metres from me.

"You ready?" I enquired.

"Ready."

Smithy remained back from the overhang. Only his rod tip came forward with a nymph dangling below it. The nymph swung precariously close to my right ear. "Careful!"

My eyes switched from fish to nymph to fish. "Out a bit," I said, "and further left. That's it! That's it!" The repetition reflecting my tenseness. "Now, drop the tip a bit — swing the nymph and drop. Don't forget to follow the current with your rod tip." Smithy had heard it all before. It had worked so he did what he was told. At close quarters there is usually only one chance, one drift, because the nymph on such a short line can drift naturally for only one arc of the rod. The nymph has to be taken before the arc is complete and the drift halts unnaturally.

The next few seconds were absolute magic for me. Smithy pushed the rod tip out once, pulled it back then swung it with even more purpose and allowed the nymph to drop at the end of the swing. It plopped just outside the overhang and a metre ahead of the fish.

"Great!" I hissed through my teeth.

The nymph sank immediately. The fish responded in an instant — not in great haste, but with absolute conviction. It drifted out into the faster water and lifted. Its jaws opened then closed with equal purpose. "Hit him," I shouted, leaving Smithy in no doubt! The rod tip whipped up then buckled down as the fish dived for the river bed. "Let him run," I barked as I scrambled to my feet. I now knew the size of the fish.

I'd enjoyed immensely the two seconds when it had come into full view, particularly because of the great size — long, broad-shouldered and fat-bellied. It is amazing how much one can observe in a short time. Smithy's fish was a jack. Its small head suggested that it was young. And it was clean — light coloured flanks devoid of obvious blemish. This was a fit trout, one that would have to be given every inch of line it demanded. Smithy understood and helped by stripping a little from the reel himself.

Really big fish like to fight right on the river bed. Usually it is a nose down, tail up battle. This fish obeyed the norm. After an initial powerful run it slowed to a steady pull upstream, exploring under every overhang, remaining as deep as possible. When it reached the head of the pool it turned, quickened its pace, and retreated downstream. Towards the tail of the pool the fish found even more energy, pushed through the shallows, then, encouraged by the fast flow of a boisterous run, took off at a tremendous rate.

Meanwhile Smithy hung on grimly, lifting rod tip and line high over menacing matagouri bushes (when he could) or using the "pass the rod around the base" technique when he could not reach over the top. Eventually, as the fish raced relentlessly on, he jumped into the current and bobbed downstream in chest deep water, rod pushed skywards. Twenty metres behind I followed the downstream procession.

Several hundred metres from where the fish was hooked I caught Smithy just as he was dragging the fish into shallow water. Those who have observed a fat fish being beached will understand. The back began to emerge, then it got higher and higher and higher! Smithy was in control now. He knew not to let the trout turn its nose back out. He kept it sliding on its belly until the water offered no more support. The fish toppled onto its side. That's when its proportions were fully revealed — undoubtedly a trophy.

An angler who wants to ensure the survival of a returned fish cannot revel in his moment of glory and admire the fish for long. I snapped two quick photos then Smithy dipped the fish's nose into the shallows. He was still gripping its tail when it thrust forward. A tremendous spray of water showered both of us as it gained depth and soon disappeared. At that moment I knew I'd have to give Smithy "a thorough listening to" that night — several times probably! I'm certain that he'd consider that we had just enjoyed the ultimate stalk.

Despite the obvious contradiction I believe I have experienced the ultimate stalk many times. On some occasions it has been the location that has made the hunt superior — under the towering mountains of Fiordland for example. At other times the clarity of the water may have added immeasurably to the experience or it may have been a particularly challenging or boisterous fish that added the extra excitement. In the context of this book the ultimate stalk awaits all anglers who hunt for their fish. It is our hope that what we have written will help to lead our readers to the pinnacle of fishing — often!

Les Hill

PART 1 : Stalking Trout

Preface to Part 1 : Location, Location, Location

One day in the summer of 1959 an eleven-year-old boy mounted his bike and cycled down Market Street, Kaitangata. At the foot of the street he crossed the railway line, turned left and pedalled off towards "The Canal," a channel that drained Lake Tuakitoto into the Clutha River. "Just fish in the canal," his parents had instructed. "Don't go near the river."

This was the first time that the lad had been allowed to fish alone. He pedalled in haste, proud, excited and overflowing with anticipation. Several other boys were already sitting above the locks on the canal and were hoisting one perch after another from the murky waters below. Our lad soon enjoyed success too. While the boys sat shoulder to shoulder they "talked fishing" and it soon became evident to the boy (not that he didn't already know) that if one wanted to catch trout then the river was the place to go — "Downstream from the dairy factory, there are heaps there!"

"Should I or shouldn't I? Should I or shouldn't I," called an inner voice. He looked towards the river. The powerful Clutha ran beautifully clear for the first time that season. The temptation would be too great for any eleven-year-old "fisherboy" who was experiencing his initial freedom. Within a short time he was clambering down a bank and pushing through a thick growth of willows. Soon he emerged into an opening in the trees and stood with the river at his feet. Ten metres out the river pushed past busily (as the mightiest river in the country does). However, nearer the shore it was slowed by a curve in the bank and spreading trees growing there.

The boy could see clearly into a broad area of water — it was about as deep as he was tall and thick beds of weed clung to the silty bottom. Between the beds lay a number of pockets. The boy liked the look of the place, and as he watched he became enormously excited. A trout hovered in one of the depressions. An older person would probably have paused, pondered a while, considered the best approach. Not our boy. In an instant his spinning lure skimmed across the water and landed outside the unsuspecting fish. As the lure was retrieved over the weed the fish pounced. A trout taking a fly is a gentle affair — with a spinning lure it's quite different. The lure is attacked. This one certainly was and the moment the trout felt the hook it sprang clear of the water and then dived for cover — but it proved no match for the lad who understood nothing about the thrill of the battle but everything about reeling a fish in quickly. No quarter was given and soon the one-kilogram fish bounced up the sandy beach. Moments later the boy fell on top of it — it was his. A quick tap on the fish's head and it was slipped into the boy's fishing bag, one of those over the shoulder types — open at each end.

Further downstream the lad found another space between willows, an elevated grassy bank — another spot he liked with a broad channel cutting into the bank. It was as he flicked his lure across the channel that he saw the swirl and the unmistakable flanks of silver. With each turn of his reel in retrieve he murmured, "Now, now, now…" and despite his absolute expectation he experienced a huge thrill when the fish struck. The boy could not believe his luck as he slipped the second fish (twice the size of the first) into his bag. The two were carefully arranged, heads down and tails sticking conspicuously out of the bag — one on each side. The journey home was to be on foot, pushing the bike slowly. More chance of being seen. And Cuddy Hale's grocery store had to be visited for three pence worth of lollies. The lollies were not important on this occasion — Cuddy Hale noticing the fish was. Hopefully he'd tell everyone. Then the boy continued up the incline home. He went, not inside, but straight to his father's office. The lad's dad, Jimmy, was the local policeman and sat behind his tall desk.

"Hello, hello — what have you got there?" the constable said knowingly, looking down his nose at his son and glancing sideways at the bag. The boy pulled the small trout out first and laid it on the floor. "What a beauty," said Jimmy. Then the bigger fish emerged. "Crikey!"

"They're very fresh looking fish for the canal," added Jimmy. Trout from the canal were usually dark coloured like the stained waters they occupied.

There was a pause. The lad didn't wish to lie to his dad. He certainly wouldn't be untruthful to the local policeman. The pause was delayed long enough for Jimmy to convey his "suspicions" — then, point made, he delayed no longer. "You'd better go and gut them and give them to your mother." The boy gathered the fish and bag quickly, keen to obey but even more eager to be elsewhere.

I know that this tale is true. The boy's name was Leslie Hill. At the age of eleven, I had been fishing for four years and was rapidly gaining an affinity with rivers and trout. While I didn't reason and think the way that I do now I was learning quickly and developing a feel for where my prospects of catching trout were greatest — developing a feel for the best locations.

In the real estate cliché, "location, location, location," the repetition is simply to emphasise a point. In the present context each word has a slightly different "meaning." The first highlights the idea of initially locating areas in rivers (or lakes) where trout probably reside. The second refers to seeking, in those areas, the most promising lies where trout may be found. The third repeat refers to the pinpointing of a fish in a lie. Locate the area, locate the lie, locate the fish. The cliché summarises (literally) a system of stalking trout and how I have endeavoured to convey the ideas in Part One of this book. The eleven-year-old boy, while not yet understanding this, was already well on the way to doing it.

Chapter 1 : Riddles Of A River

When I moved from Southland to Canterbury in 1987 I was keen to explore the new fishing waters that were available to me. I was aware that I could gain some knowledge by listening to other anglers or reading the available literature. However, I knew that the full truth would only be discovered by personal experience. I set about the task with vigour and enthusiasm. When exploring, an angler must be prepared for both success and failure. Excellent fishing will be revealed in some new waters but occasionally the opposite will be found in others. It would be usual for an author here to recount a successful visit, because fruitful forays generally make better reading. Instead the following account outlines a fishless day, and in the telling offers a few answers to some of the riddles of a river that affect the distribution of trout.

The stream was one that I had located on a map. It fed a large river, which held a good stock of trout. On that basis I figured that the stream, in its lower reaches at least, should support some fish too. I began stalking close to the mouth of the stream. Squeezing through a dense stand of willows I was confronted by a shallow stony run which carried ample water. I set off upstream, attracted by the first curve and the promise of a pool. However, there was no deep water there or on the next curve. Instead there was never more than knee-deep water. The further I pushed upstream the more despondent I became. The bed material varied little in size, consistently small in diameter and appeared lifeless. I imagined that it was scrubbed clean by frequent motion. It had the look of a riverbed turned over by the energy of each passing fresh. After a two hour upstream slog (and one can cover a reasonable distance in two hours!) I finally found a deep pool, its green hue showing from a considerable distance away. My pace slowed, expectation rose. I approached the pool from the more open side, using a sole outcrop of bedrock as a backdrop and there right in the belly of the pool drifted a good trout. I set up my gear in haste, flicked a small dry fly over the fish, which rose characteristically and took. I struck with enormous confidence. Nothing! My fly whizzed past my right ear. The fish disappeared from sight. I stood in disbelief for a moment then uttered one word to myself! Ahead the stream was shallow once more.

"Another twenty minutes," I thought. However, there were no more pools and no more trout. I retreated towards my car pondering the lessons of the day — the hope created by my map reading, the one fish occupying the only deep water exposing bedrock and the long, lifeless reaches of shallow water with an unstable, fine gravelled bed.

Features Of "Fishy" Water

The prime focus for a stalking angler is to find feeding trout. Obviously greater success will be achieved in places where the basic needs of trout are met and consequently more fish reside. Trout congregate (and that's how we like them!) where there is an abundant food supply and the security offered by deep water close by. In addition trout favour places that are punctuated by obstructions. They require well oxygenated, clear, cool water (4–19 degrees Celsius) and the streams they occupy must maintain an ample flow of water season after season. If an angler can find a place where all of these conditions (and their implications) exist then they will find trout.

River Bed Material

A river with a bed composed of small diameter, loose, unstable material (as shown by the stones on each shore). An unattractive environment for aquatic invertebrates and trout.

One of the prime requisites of good trout water, on all streams except those with a low gradient, is the presence of large, stable bed material. Large stones or rocks, with some size variation, provide an ideal environment for aquatic insects (trout food) to grow and breed — they disperse the flow in a riverbed. This is preferred by trout, providing places for them to hide, places to forage or places to hold and feed. Coarse bed material, being heavy is also less likely to be dislodged and moved when a river rises. Finer bed material (silt, sand and pebbles) does not provide the surfaces or shelter the insects, molluscs, crustaceans and small fish require and equally it is also easily and frequently displaced during freshes or floods.

A river with a stable shore and bed, composed of large diameter rocks which would not be dislodged during floods. A bed like this would provide a secure home for aquatic invertebrates, the staple food of trout.

The visual contrast between the two photographs accompanying the text is clear and reasonably self-explanatory. However, it should be noted that a stalking angler should not dismiss sterile looking beds as fishless. Trout in transit may reside there temporarily or a bed shelf or pocket may provide a feeding lie where there is sufficient food carried from a more stable bed or terrestrial source upstream in the drift. The suggestion is that a stalking angler should spend less time searching the unstable reaches and slow down where the bed looks better — that is, employ a percentage fishing technique.

Bed And Bank Vegetation

Riverbed and bank vegetation is of vital importance in providing a good trout habitat. First, plant life provides food for aquatic animals and then for the trout indirectly. The second is that it contributes stability to banks and beds while it also adds cover, protection and even feeding lies for trout in places. The accompanying photographs show clearly the contrast between an unstable river bed and those in a healthier condition.

A stream with a very unstable bed of small stones. There is an absence of deep water and the bank is largely devoid of vegetation. Poor trout habitat.

A very stable stream with abundant vegetation holding both banks and bottom growth stabilising the bed. The presence of aquatic plants suggests that the stream rarely experiences large floods. This is typical of spring fed streams. Very good trout habitat.

The presence of river bank vegetation (grasses, shrubs or forest) is evident to a stalking angler. But the less obvious river bed growth of algae is equally important, particularly when covering coarse bed material. Algal growth shows as a green or brown coloration of rocks. This microscopic plant life provides food for aquatic insects but also exists only where the bed is stable.

A river bed composed of stable, coarse material with brown coloured algal growth covering many of the stones and boulders. This is a feature of good habitat for trout.

Water Depth

No feature of a river provides better cover for trout than deep water. In small streams, pools of one metre depth with associated bank and bed cover may be adequate to support a trout population. Rivers, however, must possess extensive areas of much deeper water (two or more metres). In addition variation in depth is important — deep bellies, undercuts, drop-offs, pockets, scoured areas and so on. The variation adds to the cover provided by the deep water while it also offers respite from energy sapping flow, creating feeding lies.

An angler fishing the edge of a good pool with large boulders on the bed creating variable depth (pockets) and excellent trout habitat.

Viewing A River From Above

Having established the key physical features of good trout holding water we are poised to focus on the next chapter, the places in a river that trout are most likely to be found. However, there is some more background information that should be outlined before we move on.

The Structure Of A River (as seen from above)

While every river is quite unique and every twist and turn of each one different there are several general patterns which can be identified for an angler. Outlining some of these will help clarify what is said later. It is very rare for rivers to run naturally in a straight line for a long distance. Instead they tend to snake their way in their quest for the sea. The general

An angler casting into a typical pool in a stream, showing an eye, stomach, bank extension, pocket and tail.

pattern is for the water to flow from pool to pool — from one pool into a faster, shallower, narrower section (aptly called a rapid — or "ripple" in slower flowing streams) and into the head of the next pool. As the flow continues into the pool it deepens, widens and the current diminishes its speed into the stomach (the deepest section). Beyond the stomach the depth decreases and the flow velocity gradually increases once more as it enters the tail of the pool (the shallowest, widest — easiest to cross section). Then it narrows into the next rapid.

As a river flows through a curve the outer edge tends to be the faster flowing and more erosive side — with undercut shores very common or bedrock or boulders exposed. The inner edge is the slower flowing side, the shore on which finer sediments tend to be deposited. The nature of the flow on the inner edge is dictated by the angle of the bend through which the river flows. If the angle is wide then the flow downstream is all in one direction but when the change of direction is acute a reverse flow may develop below.

When a river does change direction a rapid will frequently be found on the upside of the bend. At the curve a shelf is often formed with the deep stomach just downstream. At the head of the pool, on the inside of the curve is an area known as the eye — an important location to be identified by stalking anglers. Where a river runs in a straight line from one pool to the next there will be two eyes at the head of the lower pool — one on each shore.

Sometimes a pool may be very long and not have great depth. Instead it may flow in one direction for a considerable distance. A section of river like this called a "reach." Sometimes the flow in a reach will be obstructed and dispersed by boulders with deeper holes created among the boulders. These deeper holes are known as pockets. It is important for a stalking angler to be able to identify pockets.

Distant Surveillance

Sometimes it can be informative and advantageous for a stalking angler to take advantage of a vista of a section of river. A broad view can convey not only much information about the river as a whole but also locate the best places to fish. Two accompanying photographs will help to explain.

A view of the Hunter River taken from high above. The most important feature of the scene is the way that the river can be seen to make its way from one side of the valley floor to the other quite regularly. This is common on rivers occupying broad bottomed valleys. For a stalking angler the importance of this is that the most stable pools, the ones most likely to hold trout, are the more permanent ones at the valley edges. The river bed tends to be less stable, with constantly changing channels, in the sections where the river crosses the valley. The best pools in these less stable sections can often be identified by the existence of shore vegetation, large immoveable boulders and deeper water. The extent and spread of the flow (whether the flow is in one or several channels) should also be a consideration. The channel with the greatest flow will usually be the one most likely to hold trout.

An elevated view of the Ahuriri River. From a vantage like this an angler may be able to make better decisions about where to begin fishing, which bank to fish from and where visibility into the water should be easiest.

27

The view that an angler gets of a river will not always be from a high vantage point. Sometimes just a short section upstream may be all that can be seen. However, even such a restricted scene may help to determine a stalking angler's approach, which shore would be the best to fish and which one to send a mate to! From a distance a fisherman should endeavour to identify: the nature of the bed material — whether it be stable, algal-covered boulders or more uniform, clean, finer material — the presence or absence of bank vegetation — the existence of pocket water — the depth — and the velocity of the flow.

Seasonal Considerations

An angler only really gets to know a river or stream after repeated visits spread throughout the year. A long-term knowledge of streams in particular is important in determining the fishing prospects. The key feature which will ultimately determine whether trout are permanent residents or not is the volume and temperature of the summer flow. Many waterways look very promising in the spring, with plenty of water (and may support fish at this time) but during the late summer and early autumn the stream may be reduced to a trickle or dry up completely.

The most stable reaches of river in New Zealand, those with the highest fish counts, are all close to the outlets of major lakes. Many anglers enjoy fishing these places and do so regularly. I prefer the other end of lakes, where the feeder streams flow in. The lower fish numbers there do not deter me. I find the smaller waters more alluring and the closeness to loftier peaks inspiring.

There is one stream at the head of one of the Canterbury high country lakes that I have fished several times. It flows through swamp and tussock, meanders through all points of the compass across a broad flat. I have never seen or caught more than a handful of fish during each of my April visits — but enough to encourage me to return. One year I decided to investigate the spring conditions and fish numbers at that time. After each of my autumn sorties I have imagined that in the spring the trout numbers would be higher, with many post-spawners remaining after the winter.

In mid-November 2003 I undertook my first early season visit, with high expectations. The flow had more purpose than I had seen previously — spring conditions. However, the water ran beautifully clear. There was no apparent reason why I should not find any fish but that's what transpired. Nothing, absolutely nothing! Either trout do not spawn there or the spawning fish had not remained (in this season at least). It may also be that the fish I have encountered each autumn have been late runners.

　　The point I wish to make though is that had I visited the stream for the first time last spring I may have been reluctant to return. It had been previous success that had drawn me back several times. This series of events emphasises the fact that an angler will learn something new on each visit to a particular place and will only gain a broad knowledge of a waterway by returning repeatedly and at different times of the year. The solutions to the riddles of a river or stream are not revealed easily — instead they are only disclosed over time. They are rationed more generously to those who put in the greatest effort.

Chapter 2 : Where Trout Choose To Dine

There's a remote valley on the West Coast that I visit often. The river there is one of my favourites and I have got to know it very well. I'm familiar with every pool, the long runs, the ripples, the rocky edges and the tributary streams. The reach outside the hut that I stay in is a beauty and invariably yields a trout or two. I was there not long ago. From the hut to the river bank was a walk of eighty metres and then there was fishing water available immediately. Against the near shore a metre or more of water pushed past purposefully. The river was falling after a fresh, slightly coloured but clearing — a very common condition encountered on "the coast." I slipped down a steep, toe toe covered bank and took a step out into the river, pushing out a little to clear my casting arm.

I endeavour to sight most fish before I cast to them. However, when conditions like those ahead of me dictate otherwise, I am quite happy to probe the water blind. Blind is perhaps the wrong word. I knew what the bed just out from the shore looked like. I knew what I was casting over. I understood my prospects. A dry fly-nymph combination is an excellent rig for fishing shallow, discoloured waters. The nymph will pass close to bed-hugging fish but the dry fly will also be visible and may tempt a rise. I pitched a Pheasant Tail and Kakahi Queen a short distance up. The nymph plopped and disappeared, the Queen settled and rode towards me. "A bit short," I thought to myself, stripped some more line free off the reel and sent the flies upstream once more. This time I'm certain that I leaned forward a little, held my rod and line out slightly straighter and fixed my eyes on the fly. One moment it rode serenely then it was gone, snatched impatiently by a fat hen fish. The suddenness of the take prompted an impulsive strike from me. Too quick I'm sure, but successful nonetheless.

Later in the day, with the sun now shining into a clearing river, I approached a stable run with a huge boulder holding firm in the flow. This was another spot I knew well and had learned to approach with great caution. More often than not, a trout would await directly ahead of the obstruction — hover with its tail almost sweeping the rock, then drift out into faster flow to intercept passing food.

As I neared the rock the sun slipped behind a cloud. The river bed disappeared. A frustrating sheen covered the water. I paused and looked skywards. It wouldn't be a prolonged wait. A fresh south-westerly would soon fan the small cloud aside. As soon as this occurred my eyes returned to the water. I shuffled along the bank at the same time — one metre, then another, then the fish appeared — right where it always was, just as expected. I stooped instinctively, sank to the ground slowly, eyes transfixed — plans to entice the fish being formulated, almost a natural part of the action. This fish and the one taken at the beginning of the day were not found by chance. The first held in a small pocket of deeper water, among some very stable boulders. I knew that the pocket was there. It never changed despite monstrous floods rearranging other parts of the river nearby. And a trout held there reliably. That's why I tensed when I had the cast right — educated anticipation.

The behaviour of these fish, the deliberate choice of a specific place to feed, is very common for trout. A knowledge of this can be most useful for a stalking angler — a knowledge of what are the likely lies (or areas in some circumstances) and an understanding of why trout choose specific places. Perhaps we should begin with the whys first.

A Trout's Needs

Trout require clean, cool, well-oxygenated water to live in. In addition they require a good food supply, provided in a place where there is security nearby — an escape from any danger that may threaten.

Deep Water

The best security for trout is deep water, however, it is even more desirable when it has other associated features. Deep water flanked and overhung by luxuriant trees like the willow is especially sought, as are pools with boulders strewn across the bed. Steep shore lines with inevitably undercut banks and fast flowing water on the top provide great cover as do dense weed beds or a tangle of sunken logs or other flood-dropped debris.

Some fish feed on the bed in deep water, three, four or five metres down — or on the surface with the same depths below. However, just as many (if not more) choose locations on the margins of deep water to feed — attracted closer to the dangers of shallow water by the abundance of food there.

Sources Of Food

I once listened to a very good dissertation by a well-known and respected Otago angler, Mike Weddell. The part of the talk I remember particularly was Mike's use of the term "food factories" for those areas of rivers and streams that produced a particularly rich food supply. He referred especially to the stable, stony, ripply areas. These usually exist at the heads of pools, but not always — sometimes they may lie along a sheltered edge of a pool or elsewhere in a stream. The important idea is that there are places that produce more food. Obviously these are attractive to trout which will congregate just downstream from "the factory."

Sometimes food will be in greater supply because it has been accumulated by the river's flow. In other instances terrestrial creatures may make their way onto a stream. Whatever the source of food trout will be appropriately placed to receive it. Trout seek food for energy. For growth to occur the intake of energy must exceed the energy expended in feeding. The understanding of this concept is important because trout feeding lies are frequently chosen partly because of their energy efficient location.

Shear Planes

On two occasions early in the past fishing season I encountered trout feeding in the fastest water in particular locations on streams I fished. The first time was in October. Several trout held in an energy sapping run right at the head of a pool. There were about five of them feeding very close together. This was a little unusual in two ways. First, trout tend to be territorial and do not usually tolerate competition close by. Dominant trout will usually chase more timid specimens away. Second, brown trout are usually lazy feeders, choosing relatively slow water from which to forage. However, on this occasion there were mayflies emerging by the thousand and these fish were each grabbing a share. Their energy intake would have easily made the effort worthwhile.

The second occasion was later in the spring, this time on a larger river. Upstream a huge "food factory," more than a hectare of stable rock-bed, produced a prolific hatch of mayflies. These emerged continually for a couple of hours and rode downstream before being sucked into two tongues of fast flow. Each tongue harboured several trout awaiting a share of the accumulating food. I stood downstream, and without guilt, took advantage of the situation!

It is more common, however, for trout to feed from places that are relatively slow flowing. The locations are carefully chosen and often quite specific. The trout will lie in relatively "quiet" water but will usually have fast water, bringing plenty of food, nearby. From their location the trout just "slip out" (or up) and help themselves to passing food then slide back and recline once more in their sheltered zone. Between the resting place and the faster water there is a very distinct change in the speed of the flow — a distinct plane which may be called a shear plane. There are two types of shear plane — lateral and vertical. Lateral shear planes are often quite visible on the surface of a river. They show in the eyes of pools and downstream of obstructions. Vertical shear planes are not visible but can be easily imagined.

Picture in your mind for a moment a small depression on the bed of a stream. The water flowing over the depression would sweep across un-impeded with almost stationary water in the "hole." The plane between the slow water of the depression and the fast water above is the vertical shear.

A lateral shear plane (the zone between the sparkling fast flowing water and the flatter, slower flowing water on the true right) showing clearly in the eye of a pool downstream from the Matakitaki River bridge.

Two trout holding in a depression with an upstream weed bed creating a vertical shear plane over the fish.

It would be easy to imagine that a trout occupying a feeding lie with a shear plane would be using either a lateral shear or a vertical shear. In fact, frequently a feeding lie will be close to both kinds of shear. A common example is a trout holding on the bed in the eye of a pool. A horizontal shear will exist down from the eye while the fish, on the bed, will be sheltered by upstream rocks.

Research Findings Related To Where Trout Feed

In 1994 two research scientists, J. W. Hayes and I. G. Jowett published a paper in the North American Journal of Fisheries Management. Their research related to the habitat use and preference by drift-feeding brown trout in three New Zealand rivers — Mohaka, Mataura and Travers.
Several findings stood out in the present context. These are listed below.

1. A very large percentage (99%) of drift-feeding brown trout occupied positions very close to the river bed.
2. A large percentage of fish (70%) fed in association with large substrate components. In the Mohaka the obstruction to flow was bedrock. In the Mataura the trout used large cobbles or depressions while in the Travers they chose boulders. The choice in each case related to what was available.
3. Brown trout fed most commonly in water which was between 0.67 and 0.86 meters deep.
4. The trout fed predominantly within a selected velocity range — 0.38 and 0.48 metres per second.
5. The fish used velocity shears (both vertical and lateral). The most common vertical shears were between 0.5 and 0.65 metres per second per metre. The most common lateral shears were much slower — between 0.02 and 0.06 metres per second per metre.
6. Most feeding forays were made within one metre of the fish and more often above the fish than to its side.

The Feeding Lies

As emphasised above feeding lies are carefully chosen by trout — from their perspective in a river. They seek out places where there is plenty of food, where they can escape quickly if danger should lurk and where they don't use excess energy. The secret for an angler is to become adept at recognising these places from the river bank. The best anglers are very skilled at doing this.

What follows is an attempt to identify the main lies that trout choose to feed from. Each one is described and most have photographic examples (some with trout on station).

Lies With A Vertical Shear

Downstream Of A Bedrock

Bedrocks are extremely varied. They vary in size, in shape, in their relationship to the surrounding bed (whether they stand alone or are part of a cluster for example) and whether they protrude from the water or are a much less obstructive part of the bed. The type being generally described here are the latter. Sometimes they may be solo but most often they lie among other rocks. Usually they are aligned across the current. Trout using a submerged rock as a feeding lie either nose right up close to the rock or "sit" a short distance downstream from it. Whether it is coincidence or not I'm not certain, but the bedrocks chosen by trout are frequently very light (and even white) in colour. I once read a suggestion that trout choose white bedrocks as the obstruction in their feeding lie because they can use the rock as a spotting board for food drifting downstream. This did not quite make sense to me because trout tend to look up for their food (and not down as a spotting board is used) and rise for it, or drift out to the sides. I cannot recall ever having seen a fish nose up to its rock as it would have to do for food slipping over it. For an angler, the good thing about trout choosing to lie with their nose on a white surface is that it renders them very visible.

A lot of trout choose to feed downstream from a rock. The benefit of being sheltered from the flow is clear and trout also favour this lie because it allows the fish to feed on the bed where much of the drifting food accumulates. Bedrock lies are also generally part of a stable river bed — an ideal environment for aquatic life to breed and grow in. Having food growing all around must be an attractive prospect for trout.

Downstream Of A Bed Shelf

Bed shelves usually exist at the heads of pools. They generally cross the bed on a slight angle at the foot of a rapid or ripple. The downstream effect on the flow is similar to what happens downstream of a bedrock, but the shear

Trout using vertical shear planes

The Lies

Downstream from a bedrock

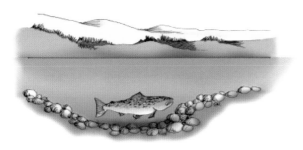

In a bed depression

Downstream from a bed shelf

Stylised water velocity profile at trout's feeding position

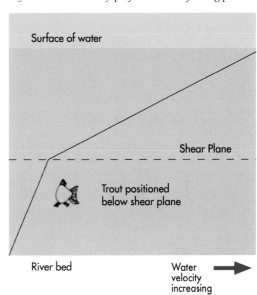

A bed shelf shows as a horizontal line across the lower third of the picture — a line delineating shallow and deep water. Downstream of the shelf a distinct vertical shear plane would exist. A trout using this shear plane would lie with its nose very close to the shelf.

zone is much more extensive. Bed shelves usually comprise less coarse bed material. Sometimes they are relatively stable but often they migrate or retreat during floods. Trout using a bed shelf as a feeding lie nose right up to the shelf (like those using a bedrock). As they feed the trout can be seen to lift or drift out to the side and often they disappear downstream into the pool behind to intercept a food item that was passing.

In A Bed Depression

Bed depressions affect the water flow in a very similar way to a bedrock. They sometimes exist in a clay or mud bed. Sometimes they may be formed by vegetation or among stones. Frequently they are found among rocks, with several rocks providing shelter from flow (rather than a solo obstruction) — and the bed ahead of the depression is not usually raised.

A trout holding on a bed shelf which has stones upstream and sand downstream (and under the fish). The trout would be holding just beneath a vertical shear plane.

Lies With A Lateral Shear

In The Eye Of A Pool

The eye occurs at the head of a pool. It is that angular corner that exists on the inside of a curve in a river. Every eye is different. Their shape is affected by many factors such as: the volume of flow, flow velocity, the angle of the curve, the nature of the bed material. Trout strongly favour the eye of a pool as a feeding lie because there is often a "food factory" just upstream and at times there will be several trout in one eye. Usually the fish will not hold right up in the corner of the eye but will feed a little further downstream and if they lie on the river bed right against the shear plane they may be difficult to see — they will be obscured by the rougher water as it rocks and rolls out of the rapid.

The eyes that I like best are the ones that exist where a river or stream turns through only a small angle. On the inner edge of the corner there is significant through flow, water tumbling over and around coarse bed material. Eyes like this will have much coarse material in the downstream part of the eye too — with numerous ideal hide-outs for trout.

The eye of a pool should be seen as an area or zone rather than a specific location. The zone can extend downstream for a significant distance on larger rivers.

An angler fishing up into the eye of a pool — one with large boulders adding to the attractiveness of the "lie" for a trout.

Ahead Of A Protruding Rock (or other obstruction)

This is quite a specific location. The rocks that trout usually sit ahead of are substantial in size and are ones that disperse significant flow. Trout that choose this lie usually sit with their tail very close to the rock behind and they hover near to the water's surface. Their zone of slower flow is small, a pressure wave caused where the flow pushes against the rock and splits and spreads to either side. I have often wondered whether trout feeding ahead of a rock feel that the rock offers some downstream security.

I have used the heading "ahead of a protruding rock." This has been done deliberately because it is normally a rock with its top high in the water column (and usually one breaking the water's surface) that is chosen. However, sometimes trout will feed ahead of a large, submerged, bedrock. The common feature is the bulk of the rocks chosen and the fact that they displace much water.

Downstream From A Protruding Obstruction

Large obstructions have a significant effect on the flow that passes around or over them. The flow is pushed outwards on each side and it is a considerable distance downstream before convergence occurs. The greater the volume and velocity of the flow then the more extensive the effect. Directly downstream behind a large rock the flow is frequently turbulent and avoided by feeding trout. However, further adrift of the rock, close to where convergence occurs, there is an area of slower flow that trout choose to feed from. In this area they have a lateral shear plane on each side.

Downstream Of A Bank Extension

There is a great variety of obstructions that extend from a bank and push out into a river or stream affecting (generally slowing) the flow. The obstruction may be a large boulder, it may be a large clod which has broken away and tumbled from the bank, it may be a tree leaning over into the water or it could be a "shingle" bar extending out (as they do at the head of most eyes).

Some bank extensions are a solid part of the bank while others are looser in their composition (like the branch of a tree or a stone bar) and allow some through flow to occur. Bank extensions allowing flow through stones or boulders seem to attract good numbers of trout on their downstream side. The slowing effect that the extension has on the current may be one factor for this but probably more significant is the presence of a "food factory" among the stones and boulders immediately upstream. Often there are tongues of more significant current in the through flow. Trout often lie right in these tongues and grab the accumulating food carried there. Similar channels can sometimes be seen among boulders or stones out on a river bed in mid-stream. These should receive a lot of a stalking angler's attention.

While most fish choose to feed downstream of bank extensions it is not uncommon for one to sit close to the shore on the upstream side. I have noticed this particularly along the margins of slower flowing streams where the obstructions are most often clumps of tumbled down bank.

An angler casting to a trout (which shows as a dark shape, circled) that feeds ahead of a large submerged rock upstream. There is a photograph of the hook-up on page 44.

Trout using lateral shear planes

The Lies

Ahead of a protruding obstruction

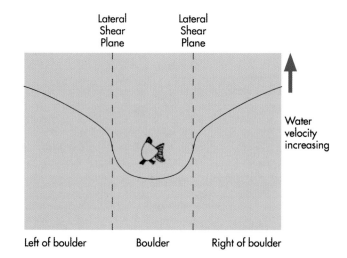

Lateral Shear Plane   Lateral Shear Plane

Water velocity increasing

Left of boulder   Boulder   Right of boulder

Downstream from a protruding obstruction

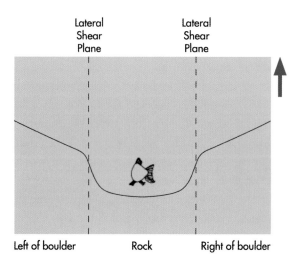

Lateral Shear Plane   Lateral Shear Plane

Left of boulder   Rock   Right of boulder

Stylised water velocity profile at trout's feeding position

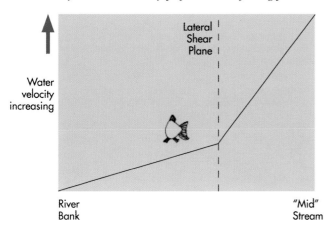

In the eye of a pool

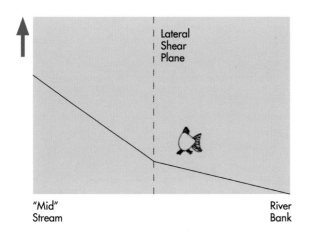

Downstream from a bank extension

The fish (being pursued on page 41) has been hooked and has sped out into mid-stream.

An angler has just hooked a trout which fed downstream of a protruding boulder. Note that the trout was feeding a few metres downstream of the boulder (as opposed to their nosing up to a bedrock) and adrift of the outer edge of the obstruction – close to a lateral shear plane.

Other Lies

Pocket Water

Many anglers would rate pocket water as one of their favourite areas to fish. Undoubtedly the success that they achieve is a major attraction. Pocket water occurs where there is a significant number of large, stable obstructions (usually boulders) in the flow. The pockets are the areas between large boulders (often protruding), bed depressions among boulders or channels of deeper water leading away from in-stream obstructions. Because pocket water is usually associated with a stable river bed then it will sit in the midst of a "food factory." This makes it attractive for trout as does the deeper water of each pocket and the protection from faster flow provided by depressions and boulders ahead or behind.

Stomach Of A Pool

As the name suggests the stomach of a pool is the central part. Like the central part of many middle-aged gentlemen it is also the more generously proportioned (deeper) section. The river's flow in the stomach is slower

An angler casting to a trout holding adrift of a partly submerged branch. The angler is fishing across the main flow and would therefore have to be very wary of line drag.

An example of pocket water. The pockets of deeper water would exist among the protruding boulders upstream of the angler.

than further up the pool. The deep water and the relatively slower flow, both contribute to the attraction for resident trout, along with the abundant food that drifts there. Dominant fish often feed in this area. While some fish do await food in the middle of the water column, most either sit very close to the surface or close to the river bed. These two places carry the most food.

Five trout feeding in the stomach of a very clear pool in a Fiordland stream.

Froth Or Bubble Lines

As a river or stream tumbles and churns through a ripple or is tossed relentlessly past numerous obstructions in pocket water a froth often forms and accumulates in lines on the water's surface as it proceeds downstream. The lines run down distinct channels or follow the dominant flow which may be displaced to one side of the river. Where the bubbles forming the froth tend to accumulate so does surface and sub-surface food. Trout obviously recognise this because they frequently sit under froth lines quite distinctly and feed on the passing banquet. I have found fishing in froth lines more productive in slower flowing streams, those that meander in places of little gradient. On streams like this froth lines follow the deepest channels close to the outer edge of curves. Likewise the trout in these streams are often found close to the shore on the outer edge — often in lies protected by lumps of eroded bank.

An angler playing a trout that was hooked as it fed in the froth line on the true left of the stream – close to the grassy bank.

At The Mouth Of A Tributary Stream

The physical nature of the junctions between streams and rivers will vary enormously but wherever one is suitable for a trout to reside in, one almost certainly will. The attractions of this location for trout are varied. It may be that a stream spills a healthy number of aquatic insects into the river or perhaps the stream may run cooler than the river it feeds. Often flood debris from the stream will push a bed or bank extension out into the river providing slower water downstream of the junction. This lie (location) can be particularly targeted by a stalking angler after a fresh — when the river is still discoloured but the tributary stream clear. A trout feeding at the junction will be visible in the small area of clear water while all other fish in the river will be lost in the murk.

Two anglers approaching an area where a backwater joins a river. The surface of the motionless backwater is distinctly different from the surface of the moving water of the parent river.

Backwater

A backwater usually exists in an old river channel. The change of channel would have occurred during a flood. A backwater is usually an area of deep, still water, connected to a river and will sometimes have a minimal inflow at its head. Trout feeding in backwaters tend to cruise in search of food (like other still water trout) and are often located by their movement. While they will venture out over shallow areas they do tend to stay close to or in deeper channels. Where there is inflow at the head of a backwater there will often be a trout "sniffing around!" A stalking angler should approach this "hot-spot" with care — particularly because the trout could be facing in any direction.

Tail Of A Pool

The tail of a pool is the widest, shallowest place at the downstream end of a pool — the place one would choose to cross a river. Because the tail is generally, relatively shallow, open and exposed it is not a favoured feeding place for the biggest fish in a pool (except from twilight onwards). However, fish do feed there — sometimes mature specimens, but more often juvenile fish. When the flow in a river becomes more boisterous during a fresh or flood bigger fish do retreat down to the tail of a pool. A stalking angler should watch out for some of these as a river falls and sight fishing becomes possible once more.

The tail of a pool may not be as important as other areas of a stream as holding water but where they are stable, having a bed of coarse material, they can be part of a "food factory" nurturing abundant aquatic insect life with feeding trout waiting a short distance downstream — in the eye of the next pool — or along the edge of the tail itself.

Undercut (Overhanging) Bank

Undercut banks are most often found along vegetated shores composed of alluvial material — the undercut being a result of lateral erosion from under the roots of plants growing above. Undercuts that trout seek usually hang over deep water or have deep water nearby and the lip of the undercut is normally close to the water's surface or even submerged.

Dual Lies

Frequently a feeding lie occupied by a trout will possess more than one physical advantage. For example, a trout holding in the eye of a pool will often also lie on the bed in a depression or downstream of a bedrock. In fact, the eyes that hold the most trout are those that have much coarse bed material. Another example is that of a trout just ahead of a rock in a pocket. While this fish will be sitting in a pressure cushion it will also be sheltered by the slower flow downstream of the rock at the top of the pocket.

Areas with multiple shear planes, as in pocket water, are particularly attractive for feeding trout and should be searched slowly (and with high expectation) by a stalking angler.

Seasonal Variations

Throughout a fishing season an angler will notice continual change — change in the flow of rivers and change in their ecology. As a result the behaviour of trout will alter — what they feed on and where they choose to feed.

The general trend of river flow is for there to be plenty of water in spring with frequent freshes keeping the temperatures low. As the more settled weather of summer prevails and foothill snows disappear river levels tend to fall — and water temperatures rise.

While rivers are fuller trout tend to feed deeper. However, as water levels fall the trout are more inclined to rise. This is encouraged considerably with the fall of terrestrial insects from December onwards.

A stalking angler should appreciate these trends and target his hunt accordingly, by searching river bed lies more thoroughly (with eyes or nymph) in spring but then expecting to see more fish in surface lies mid-season. A good example of this is the appearance of trout sitting on the surface ahead of rocks. More trout are seen occupying this lie in December and January than in October.

River Types

In early January this year I fished two contrasting rivers, each for a period of several days. One crawled ever so slowly across an inland plain of very low gradient. It twisted and turned through endless meanders and when the wind did not blow, the water's surface was devoid of ripple for long distances. The bed comprised a mixture of fine gravel and mud. It supported extensive weed beds, testimony to the stability of the flow.

The second river drained quite different country — steep, bush-clad slopes flanked the valley — and the river rushed from pool to pool, tumbling over a freestone bed. Log tangles and flood debris sitting high in the branches of trees hinted at the fury of frequent floods.

Each river supported a healthy trout population. That's why I visited them! But the way that I stalked each one was different. On the mountain river the trout were clearly "energy conscious." They fed in places where they were sheltered from fast flow — downstream from rocks, in the eyes of pools, in front of rocks — and so on. They tended to be found more often on the inside of curves — the slower side.

On the low gradient river the river's flow was never swift enough to strongly influence the feeding location of the trout. In fact, instead of feeding predominantly on the inside of curves, the trout were mostly visible on the outsides, where the current pushed hardest. This is where the froth lines ran. This is where drifting insects predominated. However, it was interesting to note that the fish still used any little flow shelter that existed — mostly eroded banks that had toppled into the stream. No wonder they were superbly fat!

These two rivers were strongly contrasted in their nature. As a result the trout behaviour was distinctly different. However, between these extremes lie other subtle differences in river characteristics and trout feeding locations. It should be of interest to a stalking angler to consider some of these variations.

While every river in New Zealand is different they can be loosely categorised — the main factors involved in producing each category being: Gradient of the bed, the amount and frequency of precipitation, the vegetation and rock type in the catchment. In my part of the country, the South Island, I can visualise six broad river types. It should be noted, however, that rarely can one stream be fitted into any one category for its entire length. Instead, most fit into one group for a few kilometres and then when the gradient changes, for example, the river's character will change and place it in a different category.

Following are my six river types with notes about the distinctive qualities and the different trout feeding patterns that may be of interest to a stalking angler.

A braided section of the Ahuriri River.

Braided Freestone Rivers

The most obvious of these are the large rivers crossing the Canterbury plains. But, there are lengths of many other rivers that are braided, with gravel beds too — in Marlborough, the West Coast, Otago and Southland. Generally braided rivers do not support large numbers of fish per kilometre. The pools that usually hold the most fish are the more stable ones on the valley margins. In the braids the best channels to fish are usually the main ones. Other stable sections are usually heralded by vegetated banks and deeper water. In these places the river gives the appearance of "resting just a little more."

While the braided, freestone rivers may not boast high fish numbers, the quality of the fish can compensate making the long walk between each one worthwhile. The fish in these rivers certainly seek to lie out of the bustling flow. The eyes of pools support many of the fish. Bed shelves and the deep water downstream harbour many others. Most fish will lie on the inner side of the main flow.

Backcountry Freestone Rivers

Unlike the braided freestone rivers these are largely confined in one channel, they have generally more stable, coarse "stoned" beds, with definite pools, rapids and runs. Most of the West Coast and north west Nelson rivers fit

A backcountry freestone river on the West Coast.

into this category, as do many of the high country rivers down the eastern side of the divide. The backcountry freestone rivers tend to be swift flowing. Because of this the trout there clearly seek feeding places that protect them from fast currents. Refuges downstream from bedrocks, deeper pockets, the eyes of pools, bed shelves and ahead of boulders are commonly used. The trout in these rivers also favour large- stoned runs and pocket water — in every sense. They will often feed very close to river banks. More fish will feed on the inner side of the main flow on a curve than opposite. Frequent, prolific insect hatches are not the norm on these rivers, consequently the trout there will feed throughout most days.

Low Country, Lower Gradient Freestone

While these rivers still have a pool to rapid to pool form they do not run with the same energy. Consequently the quite specific lies that trout favour in the high country freestone rivers will not be occupied so consistently. The trout present will still lie adrift of a variety of obstructions, seek the eye of the pool or hover in the stomach but they will also range about widely when insect life is prolific and feed in the ripples and fast runs. The trout population of many of these rivers is relatively high, but at times it would appear quite the opposite — until an insect hatch occurs. Rivers in this group are ones like those crossing the Southland plains, some east coast

A low country, lower gradient freestone river in South Canterbury.

streams like the Opihi or the Motueka in Nelson.

During a day's fishing a stalking angler should expect to cover a much shorter distance on a low gradient freestone river than on a backcountry freestone one. The longest walks are usually experienced on braided waters. Often the number of fish caught will be in inverse proportion to the kilometres covered!

A low gradient, grassland stream.

Inland Grassland Streams — Low Gradient

These streams are found in the inland basins east of the divide. They meander through rough pasture, cattle and merino country. Both shores of these streams tend to be vegetated, willow lined or overhung by tussock. Some sections of them have stable freestone beds while other lengths have gravel or mud supporting a variety of aquatic plants.

The trout in low gradient streams feed in different places than their cousins in bigger, more boisterous freestone rivers. Often they hug the shores close to tumbled-down banks, under overhangs or on the outside of and just downstream from the curve. Find a froth line and a fish will not be too far away.

Great stealth is required by anglers stalking these streams. They will often be very close to a fish before it can be seen and the fish may feed relatively close to each other. The trout respond "in force" to frequent insect hatches. They also devour the crustaceans and molluscs present and enjoy frequent falls of terrestrial insects in summer. In other words these fish are well fed!

Inland Grassland Streams — More Gradient

The main difference in the form of these streams and those above is that these are a little less stable. They run from pool to pool with one shore grassed (the outer side) and the inner edge having deposits of gravel.

When I stalk a stream like this I expect the fish to be in one of four places — right against the shore along the grassy edge, nose up to a shelf that may exist at the head of a pool, in the eye of the pool (gravel edge side) or in the stomach of the pool. The fish numbers tend to be fewer than in the lower gradient streams with greater distances walked in their pursuit.

Spring Creeks

Spring creeks tend to be low gradient, slow flowing and short in length. Their stability allows weed growth across their bed. The fish residing there use the weed as cover. They seek specific lies as strongly as in other rivers but are usually close to any deep water that may exist along the creek's length. A stealthy approach is required for what is usually "close quarters" fishing.

Categorising rivers and streams as I have done is an exercise fraught with error. There are undoubtedly hosts of situations not covered. However, by categorising, several features of rivers can be highlighted — the gradient of a river, the velocity of the flow, the depth and variation in depth of the water, the nature of bed material, the nature of banks and their vegetation. By recognising these features and evaluating their effects on a river, a stalking fisherman may be better equipped to find trout.

An inland, grassland river with more gradient than streams in the previous group.

Twenty Minutes Of Action

During January 2004, the wind seemed to blow incessantly everywhere I chose to fish. The sun shone but the wind blew — tiring conditions for a stalking fly fisherman. However, there was one day during which there was twenty minutes respite — twenty memorable minutes! Late in the morning as I battled the blow I did manage to find an occasional fish rising under banks opposing the wind, sipping from the surface between gusts. The stream I fished meandered through swampy pasture.

Around mid-day there was a sudden change. One moment I was struggling to see into the rippled water, leaning continually into the wind and gripping my hat with one hand — then it was suddenly quiet, absolutely calm. Menacing looking dragonflies materialised and skimmed over the water in abundance while their smaller damselfly cousins hovered and danced in tandem, mated in mid-flight. The stream became glassy flat. The bed lit up and a whole new world appeared — weed beds aplenty

A West Coast spring creek.

swayed in the gentle flow and trout were there too. I swear that from where I stood I could see five nearby. They fed as if they had been doing so all day — drifted just below the surface sipping small mayflies that had arrived too.

Two bends of the river away, my brother Ho and Len Cook fished. I could not help but notice a change in their demeanour. Gone was their forward tilt. They no longer had one hand on their hats. In fact they were side by side on their knees with one of them waving his rod about frantically — a sure sign that a fish was about to be molested.

My attention was diverted for a short time only. A fat fish sipped noisily close to my feet. I was on my knees in an instant too awaiting the chance to flick a fly discreetly in its direction. During the next twenty minutes I rose four fish. As the second of the two that came to shore was released another rose temptingly upstream. My grin was as wide as the stream. I had visions of afternoon long action. However, as quickly as the calm had prevailed it vanished. First there was a puff of breeze, then the gusts grew in strength and frequency. The bed of the stream faded from sight. The trout disappeared, as did the dragonflies and their friendly relatives. I was soon looking for more banks opposing the wind, hoping to find a fish rising in the relative calm, in the only feeding lie out of the wind. More often than not, stalking anglers have to adapt in this way. More often than not, they will encounter less than ideal conditions and have to target the best places in the given circumstances. That's the reality of trying to find trout where they choose to dine.

Chapter 3 : The Elusive Image

While every river is different, neighbouring waterways often share common characteristics. This is logical since they should be fed by similar rainfall patterns, drain congruous terrain, flow over related geological features and presumably emerge from catchments covered by like vegetation. The larger rain (and snow) fed rivers of the West Coast, south of the Taramakau certainly possess a number of similarities. They are all relatively short, they are swift, gather their volume quickly from numerous side streams and most of all are flood-prone. As a result they tend to have unstable beds — yet they do support trout — not large numbers, but sufficient to attract a fisherman with the energy to match that of the environment. Often an angler will search a long stretch of water and find no fish and then discover several in one reach. This pattern was reinforced to me in the summer of 2004.

I was exploring a section of river that I had not investigated previously, in the Hokitika catchment. I began the stalk immediately upstream of a particularly boisterous and uninviting run (for angler and trout). But the water ahead appeared unstable too, with little depth — just an occasional pocket. Each was scrutinised with care and I even probed occasionally with a nymph, hoping to lift a fish from an obscured lie. They were, however, probes possessing little conviction. My view into the water was quite clear.

As I moved upstream I checked every possible lie but also continually looked well ahead — watching for hints of water more likely to hold trout. I was searching for shores clothed in stabilising vegetation, shores composed of rocks rather than stones. I also sought signs that deep water was more likely to exist as indicated by variable water gradient and surface features like extensive areas of flat water being passed by stronger mid-stream flow. Deeper water is also often found at a curve in a river with a higher bank on the outer shore. Banks like this are often visible hundreds of metres away.

More than a kilometre of water had been passed before I approached a reach with real promise, one that slowed my progress to a shuffle. Moss and lichen-covered rocks stretched from pasture to the water's edge and beyond — the tops of many emerging from the water along the margins of a deep run. The richer blue-green colour of the water showed its depth.

A stalking fisherman who has passed a long length of sterile water becomes extra cautious when his hopes soar. My shuffle slowed and eventually I paused. I am continually reminded, when stalking, how much more a stationary angler sees — even in twenty or thirty seconds.

I was no longer looking well ahead but focussing just beyond casting distance. And for me that is not very far! A small bed depression, an ideal niche for a trout, protected by a large, flat bedrock on its upstream margin held my attention. I watched and watched, eyes unwavering. I knew that if a trout resided there (which seemed highly likely) it would show eventually. And it did.

One moment there was nothing then a shape appeared, lifted from camouflage on the dark bed, intercepted a nymph mid-column then dropped from view once more. It was visible for about three seconds — no more. Instinctively I sank to my knees, instantly considering how to catch it.

A Strategy For Finding Trout

The brief sequence of events described above leading to the discovery of a trout hopefully conveys a message that rivers are not just a pattern-less stream of flow but, in fact, do possess a degree of structure which can be read to an extent by an angler. The structure is certainly understood and utilised by energy efficient, wary trout. During a stalk anglers should be continually searching, near and far, for clues that may help in their quest.

Spotting trout is, to me, one of the most important skills an angler can possess for consistent success. Some anglers, even after years of fishing have difficulty locating all but the most obvious fish. The eyes of others instinctively seem to find even the most subtle images amid the jumble of ripples and rock. I enjoy the hunt as much as the catch. There's a great thrill in spotting a feeding fish. Part of the fun no doubt is the knowledge of the contest ahead. The hunt is not just a simple matter of looking for fish — in fact, that is the final act.

The beginning of the hunt, when I first approach a river as described above is to look upstream and down and survey the whole scene. I believe the modern jargon would say — "to look at the big picture!" When fishing new waters in particular I assess the stability of the banks and bed, search for deep waters and generally look for the areas most likely to hold trout. With this in mind I contemplate which side of the river offers the better prospects, assuming I can cross. As I work upstream (stalking anglers

usually move upstream) I continually check ahead looking for the places to tarry later — this continues throughout a day's stalking.

With "the big picture" considered a stalking angler can select those areas that should be worthy of brief inspection and those that should receive much attention, that is the waters that should be searched long and hard — the high percentage places.

While passing the low percentage areas (the areas less likely to hold trout and those that should receive less attention) I still focus on the water, particularly on rivers with higher fish densities. Every piece of water has the potential to hold a trout and most do at some time — even if it is a fish in transit or one that has been displaced. However, when adjacent to an area with high promise I linger more. Initially I don't search specifically for trout but seek out the most likely lies — identify the pockets, the deeper runs, the obstructions to flow — and so on. Then I focus intently on these one at a time, looking — not usually for a whole trout — but for a hint that one feeds there.

A downstream view of a stream illustrating how different areas and flows show from a distance.

A stream with a high, steep bank on one side and a shore with a gentle gradient on the other. The true left, with coarse, algal covered material shows as the area most likely to hold trout.

What To Look For

There are a couple of pools on the Hurunui River that I visit several times each year. As I approach the first, the initial view of the water is down from a lofty cliff top. If the trout are out and feeding they show very clearly drifting about close to the surface. In the second pool, a few hundred metres upstream, the fish are also quite obvious as I look from an elevated position. Similarly I can picture numerous situations where trout are easily spotted — drifting about in clear, slow-moving pools or sipping from glassy, windless surfaces. However, finding trout is most often not so easy. Usually images are disguised and camouflaged — merged with mottled, stony beds, shrouded by the surface disturbance of flowing water or masked by the effects of changeable weather — wind, rain, cloud and sunshine. Usually what a stalking angler is looking for in ripples, runs and pockets, is a hint of a trout, or more accurately, several hints — subtle images that combine to suggest a fish lies ahead.

Two trout holding in a pool. The images are reasonably typical of what an angler can expect to see. They blend with their surrounds and are fudged by water surface movement.

Line

To an inexperienced eye a river bed may appear an unordered mass of stones, boulders and other debris. But this is not so. River bed material is all eroded, shaped and deposited by the energy of flowing water and the bed of each river does acquire some natural lines, augmented by (largely microscopic) plant growth. When a trout lies and feeds above a river bed it also adopts a natural position (or body line) — an even more definite and consistent one than that of the debris below. Trout, being very energy efficient, always line up their torpedo shape (when holding in the flow awaiting food) exactly in line with the direction of flow. The line is a very natural one and is often distinct to a trained eye from other textures in the river. Shapes that do not line up with the current can be quickly dismissed.

Sometimes a trout may appear to hold on the bed at a slight angle to the current. Where this does appear, one can be certain that there will be an obstruction, a bed ridge or something that is pushing the flow there at an angle and the fish is aligned accordingly.

Shape

Trout have a distinctly elongated torpedo-like shape. When the line of a fish shows in the current so will part of its shape. Interestingly stalking anglers usually focus their gaze on a particular depth at any one time. And when the bed is the focus trout mid-column or near the surface can escape attention. Most actively feeding trout will hold at least a little off the bed. With this in mind it is usually better to focus for shapes and lines in the water column rather than at the base of it.

Fins

When attracted by a shape lined up in a likely lie I immediately watch for more evidence that a trout has been spotted. Usually the next clue sought is the presence of fins and a caudal (tail) fin in particular. The tail fin will sometimes "stand out" because of a distinct, black (vertical) edge. Dark rays may also exist on the pectoral or pelvic fins and show as they move subtly as stabilisers. The dorsal fin may also stand out. These may appear tiny things to look for, however, they can be the difference between distinguishing a trout or not. There are occasions, particularly along the margins of slow flowing streams or in the shallows of backwaters (or ponds), when the first indication that a trout lurks near will be the very subtle image of its dorsal fin or the tip of its caudal fin cleaving the water.

A trout holding on the surface of a stream near to the shore. The tips of its dorsal and caudal (tail) fins are out of the water.

Colour

Like most fish, trout tend to be dark on their dorsal surface and lighter underneath. Usually stalking anglers will be looking down upon their quarry, at the darker back. Sometimes the dark shade will be almost black or dark grey, but the colour can vary from blue-grey to a deep green.

Trout have the ability to change their colours to match that of the environment they live in. An example of this is the change in colour of trout from a silver when they enter a river from the sea to a darker shade when they have resided in the fresh water for some time.

Colour can be the clue that a stalking angler first sees when spotting a trout. Sometimes it may be a flash of white when the fish turns or rolls seeking food or opens its mouth or sometimes it will be an elongated green, blue or grey back — a colour aligned naturally with the current.

Many years ago Chappie Chapman described to me the subtle image that appears in a stream (the only clue distinguishing a trout's presence) as a smudge. The term is a very apt description of all that often appears, particularly in clear, ripply water — a grey smudge. Usually a fish that shows as a smudge is light in colour, the tone of a healthy trout. Darker trout — the ones often seen very close to the edge of a stream, in shallow waters or in unusual lies are generally poorer specimens showing signs of stress.

An angler casting directly upstream to the nearer of two trout. Both show as smudges beneath the wind riffled surface.

Shadow

Earlier I suggested that trout will be spotted more readily if an angler is focussing at the right depth in the water column. This has been stressed to me on a number of occasions when I have located a fish by spotting its shadow first. Usually when this happens I am aware that what I am looking at has the right alignment and the right shape but nothing more. However, an adjustment in the height of focus usually brings the fish into view — and sometimes remarkably clearly. Obviously this is a fine day clue.

Movement

A green-backed shape lodged downstream from a flow obstruction or a shape lined up naturally in a river's flow are clues that a trout may have been located — clues that require continued attention. However, proof that a trout lingers ahead is when a movement is seen. It may be as subtle as the movement of a fin, the opening and closing of a mouth, the gentle waving of a caudal fin or the slide of a shadow across a bed. Most often the disclosing motion is the trout shifting sideways or lifting to feed.

Whatever the movement seen it is invariably a significant moment in a stalker's day — one that induces a brief nod and mental, "Yes!" — a moment of excitement, realisation of the possibilities ahead. The smudge alluded to earlier is a hint of a trout most often seen in joggled runs, places characterised by partial images. The smudge that is seen is often not the shape of the fish as it moves but the covering and uncovering of images as the fish moves past them. The actual image of the fish in water with an agitated surface is usually only revealed briefly as one of a procession of moving surface windows passes overhead.

When searching waters with a waving surface I endeavour to find a moving window and follow it with my eyes as long as it exists. They change constantly, grow in area or get consumed by surrounding turmoil.

The window, a small, transparent area of flat water, will offer a brief, clear glimpse into the waters below — a momentary snapshot, but revealing nonetheless — sufficient to allow an angler to spot a trout.

A trout taking a surface fly causing surface disturbance. In this instance it is a large fish but causing only a small ripple. This is not uncommon.

Riseforms

Another movement which can suggest that a trout is feeding nearby is water surface disturbance. Sometimes the disturbance may be quite subtle — a bulge of the surface caused by a fish intercepting a nymph below. At other times the surface will be broken. The break may be just the tip of a trout's nose or it may be a porpoising motion with the nose emerging first followed by the tip of the tail moments later. Some trout signal their presence with a flourish by leaping clear of the water, returning with a very loud splash — an action characteristic of juvenile trout.

The take of a surface fly can sometimes be accompanied by a very audible sucking sound as an insect is pulled down. It is not unusual for a take like this to be heard before it has been seen.

Bow Waves

Bow waves pushed ahead and out by trout as they move in shallow water are usually observed when trout have been alarmed and are speeding away seeking the security of deeper water. However, sometimes a feeding trout will reveal its presence with more subtle, slower moving waves or darting waves created as mobile sub-surface food is pursued. The presence of a trout may be conveyed to an angler in a variety of ways. Therefore it is necessary to train ones eyes to look not just for the shape of a fish but equally for the other signs too — a smudge, a rise-form, a movement, a fin and so on. An awareness of what to expect undoubtedly leads to more success.

Trust Your Instincts

A few years ago my brother, Ho, and I were stalking up a small stream in the late spring. It was one of those streams that held small numbers of fish, about one in every second pool — but those that resided there were healthy specimens.

We'd landed perhaps a couple of fish in the morning and approaching mid-day we came upon an inviting ripply run, one that pushed down busily over a coarse, stable bed. Ho was ahead, the spotter. I lingered some distance adrift, aware that two anglers side by side were more likely to scare fish than one dictating his own pace and line along the bank. My attention was far from the river when Ho called — "Up here! There's one near the bank."

I was soon at Ho's side. "Where?" I enquired. Using his rod as a pointer, Ho directed my eyes to a shape, lined up nicely in a deeper run. "Seen it move?" I asked.

"Came to the top once," said Ho. "Have a go."

The surface of the stream jostled and rolled along, obscuring visibility into the water somewhat, distorting and moving images too. The, "Came to the top," encouraged me. Without delay, or further inspection I sneaked back along the shore then entered the water downstream of the fish. In the busy water I was able to get reasonably close before casting. First I drifted a little dry fly over the shape which I could see quite plainly. No interest was shown. Next I tried a small nymph. Then it was a heavier nymph and another and another. "You sure it's a fish?" I asked. In the wavy water the shape did appear to move a little, but with each passing minute (and nymph!) I became less and less convinced.

"I'll have a closer look," said Ho, a hint of doubt in his tone. He moved nearer, then nearer — head pushed forward, eyes willing a clear image of a fish to emerge. However, the closer he got the more his demeanour revealed the truth. "Sorry," he offered, "it's a rock."

As we moved on to the next pool I couldn't resist making a comment. "What did it take from the top?" There was no response! The lesson that an angler could take from this incident (which all stalking anglers could identify with I'm certain) — could be that we should identify fish quite clearly before casting to them. However, I'm reluctant to adhere to this belief. I'd suggest that anglers should trust their instincts and if there is a hint that a fish lies awaiting then it should be approached as a fish — approached with caution, fished to without delay. A large percentage of the time one's instincts (being fuelled by observations and experience) will not deceive or betray us. Usually when we think a trout is lurking, it will be. To move forward a little or sneak closer to a river's edge to verify a sighting would most often be counterproductive, with the fish scared. Remember that what a fisherman seeks is a very elusive image.

Chapter 4 : Tread Softly, Tread Slowly

Occasionally each season I come across a trout feeding very close to me before I have spotted it — not because I was inattentive or negligent but because the fish resided in a unique place. The situation would usually be one where I was forced to stalk very close to the water's edge, confined by dense streamside vegetation or a steep bank — and, at the same time, the trout would feed near the bank. I enjoy finding a trout in a place like this. I like being able to observe very clearly the trout's behaviour but also relish the challenge of pursuing the fish without causing alarm.

Last summer I came across a healthy looking brown feeding within a metre of the bank I stalked along. It had chosen a very protected lie, one formed downstream by a massive beech tree which had been deposited by flood waters, left with its roots against the shore and its thick trunk pushing out into the flow. As a result a pocket of very slow flowing, almost stationary water existed adrift of the log — a little "pond" about ten metres long. The beech was not the only flood debris there. Another trunk had toppled from the shore, hanging out precariously above the trout's home.

I was no more than two metres from the fish when I first spotted it. I pushed my head out through some dense scrub and looked into the deep water just below my feet. At the same instant the fish's snout broke the water's surface as it took a fly. I tensed immediately, dared not even blink. The fish, however, remained fluid in its motion, pushed ever so slowly away from me, under the overhanging limb and on towards the head of the "pond." Twice more it sipped from the surface before reaching the end of its territory then it turned, dipped out into deeper water and disappeared. A short time later it reappeared at my feet, then commenced another patrol upstream. Concealed among bank-side scrub, I relaxed for some time, enjoyed watching the fish repeatedly patrol its territory taking any food encountered en route — morsels nudged from the bed, nymphs intercepted mid-column and flies pulled down from the surface. This was a fish with seemingly catholic tastes. However, while I watched I was also contriving to deceive it. Obviously the difficulty that faced me was how to get a fly onto the water without being seen, how to drop a fly from my scrubby hide and out through leafy limbs.

From where I stood it would have been relatively simple to poke my rod out over the water and dangle a fly down on a metre or so of line — make the drop when the fish fed further up its beat, then wait for it to return as had been its habit. But, the rod would have been exposed and probably cause alarm. The alternative approach was to shift a few metres upstream to where the trunk hung out over the water and use the cover this provided.

The fish passed "under my feet" once more then pushed ahead in search of food. When it neared the far end of its beat I shuffled towards the trunk — gained as much ground as I dared before pausing in a new hide. Then I waited. The fish duplicated its pattern of turning into deeper water and dropping from sight before reappearing to repeat its run. At the appropriate moment I made a little more ground towards the trunk then paused, awaiting another opportunity. Twenty, perhaps thirty minutes elapsed before I crouched at my destination — then when the moment was right I laid my rod along the thick limb where it rested concealed from below. Next I allowed a tiny fly to fall onto the water on two metres of fine tippet.

Observing a fat trout sip a natural fly from the water just a few metres away in very clear water is a fine moment for a trout fisher, but observing closely the same fish engulf one's own fly is singularly animating, an act willed, incited, encouraged by the angler then watched in momentary wonder when it actually occurs. This angler clung to a scrubby branch with his left hand, leaning precariously towards the water, and clutched rod and line in his right. When the fly had disappeared and the fish closed its jaws the one handed strike was made.

Not all trout have to be approached with the same stealth as the one described above. Most feed in more open locations and further away. However, whatever the situation, anglers must be ever cautious, always conscious that the trout must never be made aware of their presence before a fly is presented.

Stalking trout — the act of finding fish before fishing to them — can be viewed like a sport or game. In this respect "the game of stalking" comprises both defensive and offensive aspects — a game of "hide and seek." The approach to the fish just described was largely defensive with great care being taken in remaining concealed, using cover and very slow movement. However, the focus of actually finding and spotting fish embodies a number of offensive aspects. The discussion that follows will use the analogy to clarify the points highlighted.

Defensive Aspects Of Stalking

No matter what the quarry may be — deer, pig, goose, snapper or trout — their most successful hunters all consider the defensive features of a stalk very carefully. Defence is the foundation of stalking. Those hunting deer or pig are aware that the animals they seek have a well-tuned sense of smell. These hunters read the wind carefully in an effort to minimise the chance of their scent reaching their quarry. Goose hunters seek a bird with very keen eyesight. Hides placed in a variety of depressions or among vegetation are often covered with camouflage nets to hide the gun bearers beneath. Snapper fishers, angling in shallow water from a boat, endeavour to avoid excessive vessel floor noise which can scare the fish below.

Trout fishermen hunt a creature with a very acute sense of smell, a well developed ability to feel vibrations in the water and excellent eyesight. All of these senses are used by trout to warn when danger lurks near, so a brief outline of pertinent details will help when considering the defensive aspects of a stalk.

A Trout's Senses

Sight

Trout use their eyesight more than any other sense in detecting danger. Their eyes are placed dorsally on either side of their head which allows them a very wide field of view, both laterally and above. Their field of view is much greater than that possessed by humans. Apart from an inability to see what lies below them (which has little relevance in the present context) trout have only a small zone behind them that lies out of their sight. They appear to be particularly alert to objects above and can see elevated objects behind them.

For a stalking angler two aspects of a trout's eyesight are particularly important. First, they are particularly sensitive to movement. Stationary objects may at times go unnoticed but any motion is soon perceived. It seems that the faster the movement the stronger the reaction to it. I have often seen trout dive for cover when a bird (or the shadow of one) has passed over the water nearby. Also trout possess a demonstrated ability to detect contrast — contrast in colour, brightness or shape. Trout are able to see objects both close up and a considerable distance away. Exactly how far outside the water they can see I'm not certain but if a body is highly contrasting (like an angler on the horizon) and moving then the distance may be forty, fifty metres or more. Trout do see colour. This has obvious implications for fly tiers or anglers when choosing what lure to use but its implications are important for a stalking fisherman too.

Smell

Very recently I was reminded that trout have a very well developed olfactory system and use it to detect foreign odours in the water. I was stalking upstream along a tightly wooded brook. As I approached the head of one pool I sighted a trout feeding right against a shear plane, on the shore side of the fast flow. As I dropped into the stream (which was necessary for me to cast) I noticed that I stood in a backflow, one that drifted upstream against the shore, then curled out towards where the fish fed. A quick estimate of the water speed suggested that I had less than a minute to entice the fish before my scent would reach it. I had the fly in the air in an instant and dropped it equally hastily. It drifted over the fish which lifted just a little — a movement of recognition only. There wasn't time to change my fly so up the pattern went again. It drifted past without reaction. Then a natural was taken from the surface and a nymph soon after. I was about to cast again when the inevitable occurred — the fish darted for cover. When they see danger trout will often ease away slowly and fade into deep water but foreign smells will usually evoke a hasty retreat — as it did on this occasion.

Sound

Trout usually react strongly to foreign sounds too. They have two detection systems — their ears buried on either side of their head and they possess the ability to detect low frequency vibrations through their lateral line (a line which is quite visible running along the entire flank of the fish). Sounds (like voices) in the air are not perceived by trout but vibrations emanating from river bank or bed certainly are.

Using The Knowledge About The Trout's Senses

Probably the most significant defensive strategy that a stalking angler can employ is to *tread slowly* in his quest for fish because trout use their perception of movement to detect danger more than any other means. However, this does not suggest that the passage upstream should be uniformly deliberate and lingering but a journey that slows when waters very likely to hold fish are being passed and accelerate along low percentage waters.

There is more care needed than just moving slowly if a stalking fisherman wishes to avoid detection by ever-wary trout. The distance from the stream shore that the angler stalks is also most important. A simple guide that I use is to walk the maximum distance from the shore that allows good visibility into the water. In favourable conditions this may mean that I stalk along a line well back from the bank. This demonstrates an appreciation of a trout's ability not just to see movement but also its capacity to determine contrasts. The further back that an angler stalks then the slower his relative movement will appear and the more subtle the contrast in shape and colour.

An angler searching the water from a concealed position, back from the bank edge and in the shade.

By wearing clothing in colours and tones matching a river's surrounds (vegetation in particular) an angler further diminishes the contrast his riverside presence offers. Obviously concealment can be further enhanced when a stalking fisherman hovers behind conveniently placed cover — a riverside gorse bush, luxuriant tussock or heaped up flood debris. Where a choice exists a stalking angler should proceed upstream by going around behind riverbank cover rather than the outer side. It is always tempting to take the exposed route because the water remains in sight — but the objective "of the game" — to see fish before they see you — should be continually foremost in mind. When vegetation is being used as back cover some concealment is effected particularly if the angler moves slowly and close to the cover and the obstruction stands several metres or more away from the river's edge.

A stalking angler who would have two options when continuing upstream — either by moving around the gorse bush on its river side or behind the bush. The second option would be the better (more defensive) choice.

Utilising available shade and adopting a low profile also diminishes the contrast between anglers and their surroundings — reducing the chances of being detected by a resident trout. It is quite natural for anglers to proceed up a river with their rods held ahead. While they are in view they can be weaved past vegetation more safely. But it should be remembered that if a rod is pushed ahead then this will be the first thing that emerges into a trout's vision — a point worth considering particularly when stalking along an elevated position and close to the river bank. Ideally a rod should be carried low and pointed away from the river.

Frequently when a trout has been spotted an angler will wish to retreat before casting. I believe that the best line of retreat is back along the path just covered. The reason for this is that if the trout did not see the approach in a particular way then it is less likely to see the reverse movement than one in another direction. I also believe it is better to retreat by walking backwards, rather than turning around and walking away. In turning an angler's shoulders swing relatively quickly while a backpack will invariably contrast in colour to the front profile offered moments before. Variations in movement, shape and colour are noticed very readily. Thoughtful stalkers will continually consider how they can diminish or eliminate such signals.

Commonly, anglers will stalk in pairs. There are both advantages and disadvantages to a team approach. The advantages are greater once a fish has been spotted and it is "being lined up" by a fisherman ready to cast. The disadvantages are that two anglers on the bank present twice the image, twice the movement, twice the chance of signalling the presence of danger

76

unless their conduct is co-ordinated. Usually it is safer for one angler to do the spotting with the other staying well behind. Often when two anglers together do spot a trout there is a temptation for one to point out the fish to the other — an action that can involve fast hand or rod movement, the kind of contrast noticed by trout.

Stalking anglers should be continually aware of the position of the sun and how this will affect the image that this presents to trout in the river ahead. An obvious caution is to avoid casting a shadow (body or rod) onto the water. This is particularly relevant early or late in a day when shadows are longer. How we are illuminated can be important. It may seem logical that we would stand out more with the sun on our back, presenting a silhouette. However, the many photographs that I view of anglers streamside suggest that one lit front on (even in overcast conditions) shows more clearly. Because stalking trout is most often an upstream pursuit the fact that trout can detect a wading angler's scent very readily is usually irrelevant. But when there is a danger of a fisherman being exposed by scent when wading in a back current or two anglers share one stretch of river for example, ways to diminish or eliminate the danger should be considered.

The need for hunting fisherman to *tread softly* needs little explanation. The chances of sending a trout diving headlong for cover through heavy footfalls is greatest when large loose boulders are being crossed or when stalking with a quarry nearby. Anglers who respect the wariness of trout and are instinctively cautious will rarely signal their presence with clumsy footwork.

Another Reason For Caution

Fishermen who are fortunate enough to spend a lot of time riverside will have noticed that trout react differently to "approaching" anglers at varying times during a season. There are occasions when they can get quite close, put their line on the water and present flies without causing undue alarm. However, at other times trout will flee from someone approaching even a long distance away or will react to a fly line before it has even placed a fly on the water. Generally the wariness of trout increases as a fishing season proceeds (but I have often encountered uneducated fish being very "flighty" on opening day) and as conditions brighten in summer and rivers fall.

What does seem apparent to me is that trout often detect much more than they react to. One could assume that an uneducated trout would not see subtle signals (like a moving bush or fly line or artificial fly on the water) as significant danger. However, having been caught once the same fish would more probably react to the unusual. A fish caught several times would be the one which demonstrates how much fish do actually see — a surprising amount. It is probable that stalking anglers who treat all fish as being educated will experience greater success than those who are less vigilant.

Offensive Aspects Of Stalking

There is little point to anglers sighting trout if they have been spotted by the fish first. Usually trout that have detected danger will cease feeding and seek cover and be unavailable for some time. Because of this the defensive aspects of stalking should take precedence over the offensive ones — anglers should use all of their guile to *tread softly and slowly* and then actively seek undisturbed fish.

One of the most important defensive ploys that stalking anglers should use is to move slowly. This doubles as an offensive action too. While trout detect our presence from contrast or movement we also observe them via the same signals. These signals are more apparent to fishermen who are stationary or have a window ahead which is changing very slowly only. To spot trout efficiently anglers should keep their eyes focussed on (or through) the water without distraction. By doing so they have an uninterrupted and continuous image and are better able and quicker to notice contrasts. Maintaining absolute focus on the water can be relatively

Two anglers pausing for a while, searching the water ahead for signs that a trout may feed there.

easy along a shore which is even underfoot, however, over boulder-strewn ground or through lush vegetation moving without watching one's feet can be more hazardous. Usually I endeavour to move so slowly that I feel my way with my feet but where I cannot achieve this I stop frequently to survey both bank and river.

Frequent pauses, particularly alongside promising waters, can reveal much that would have been missed by anglers who had not tarried. Water that had seemed fishless can suddenly be found to harbour a trout hiding on the bed or a pool that appeared to support one fish can prove to hold two or even three. Fishermen who are not moving will be better able to see movement or subtle contrasts in front of them.

The surface of a stream is changing constantly. In places and at times it is absolutely transparent, but often it can be quite the opposite — glassy, mirror-like, hiding all that lies below. Glassy surfaces are encountered more frequently early and late each fishing season and at the beginning and end of a day. They are also more prevalent in places backed by a low horizon and in partly cloudy or overcast conditions. Stalking fishermen can use two principal ploys to combat the surface glare of a reflective water surface — they can search from a more elevated position (altering the viewing angle into the water) or seek high backdrops to the water being looked into (effectively raising the horizon ahead). Very often a favourable backdrop (the darker the better) will not stand conveniently across and upstream of fishermen but be at right angles to their movement. A backdrop like this can be used but because it allows visibility into the water to the angler's side (and not ahead) they must stalk well back from the water's edge. Rarely do we encounter ideal stalking conditions with unhindered visibility continually into a stream. Consequently an upstream stalk usually involves walking at constantly varying distances from the shore and looking into the water from all angles — downstream, side on and even upstream in places. All can be successful, particularly for defensive stalkers.

An angler using a very elevated position to look into the river below. While the position would allow good visibility into the water it would be important for him to move slowly and to stay back from the bank edge to diminish the chance of being seen by trout.

Whether a day is sunny or overcast it is the sun which illuminates a river bed and its occupants. A little thought about some aspects of what effect this has can help. It would seem logical that stalking with the sun behind would be the best situation because the sun would fall directly on a fish. Often this works in our favour (with the fish showing in more detail and lighter in colour) but sometimes it can hinder our view. One obvious situation when the sun lighting up all ahead is a disadvantage is when a bright backdrop is in front — one covered in light coloured vegetation or light grey stones or rocks. These reflect on the water causing unhelpful glare. When we look into a river with the sun opposing us we can expect to find fish which are illuminated on the side hidden from us. It's worth knowing and expecting this because what we can anticipate is a darker image — more shaded flanks.

The behaviour of trout varies with changing river conditions and seasons. Thoughtful stalkers should consider the conditions encountered. Having an inkling of what to expect at a given time can be an advantage. For example, during spring time rivers generally carry more (cooler) water. While these conditions prevail trout tend to feed deeper. Logically stalking fishermen should focus their attention more on river bed lies. In mid-summer some trout seek more surface food and sit higher in the water column. They tend to be found ahead of obstructions more often than in spring. Many trout are attracted into the ripply water at the heads of pools at the height of summer. In autumn many trout become more active and visible in the afternoon. Knowing this I often don't begin stalking until after lunch or I'll sit with an elevated vista of a pool waiting for some activity to show.

Many anglers begin thinking about a day's stalking long before reaching a river. They consider carefully where they will fish according to the conditions on a given day. For example on a partly cloudy or overcast

The effect that a high, dark backdrop has on reducing glare is shown in this picture. The view into the water from the photographer's position is much better on the right side of the frame and poor on the left where a low horizon lies behind. An angler stalking upstream should be continually looking for high backdrops to assist visibility into the water.

day they may choose to fish a river which runs through tighter terrain or is flanked by tall vegetation on both banks. In locations like these stalkers would encounter less front glare and better visibility into the stream. On bright sunny days more open locations may be preferred because light toned low horizons would not hinder visibility. Also early and late on a sunny day, tree lined shores can become shaded, hindering a view into the water. On a windy day it makes sense to seek a place with the wind on one's back. This may not necessarily assist a stalk but it will certainly allow easier casting and render the outing more pleasant. If the location is chosen carefully some shelter from the wind may be found and fish located more easily.

Weather is not the only condition contemplated prior to heading streamside. River conditions will also receive attention as will knowledge about where there are likely to be plenty of fish at a given time of the year.

There is much to contemplate. I have only outlined a few considerations here, a small number of the possibilities stalking fishermen could consider to add to their success in finding fish. However, in doing so I hope that I have highlighted and emphasised that stalking is more productive if a thoughtful approach is adopted — an approach which involves an understanding of the behaviour of trout, an awareness of the conditions that are (or may be) encountered on a river and an ability to continually adapt and change the approach around every corner of a stream.

There is one more aspect of stalking I believe is important and should be mentioned. When stalking anglers should *expect to* find fish. Rather than contemplating whether one may feed ahead, consider where it will be and how many others will be found nearby. By expecting to find fish one will. Anglers who adopt the same attitude to catching trout rarely fail, particularly if they tread softly and tread slowly.

Chapter 5 : A Still Water Diversion

I cannot remember having ever told someone else's fishing story. I've avoided the ease with which one could be trapped into deviating from the truth by doing so — and anglers seem to stray in this manner regularly! However, I've heard the tale of my brother's landing of a six kilogram, lake-edge fish so many times that I believe I can almost retell the story more accurately than he can, although mine will be a less animated version.

The story is recalled in the first person, but on this occasion the "I" is Ho and not me. While the sun shone brilliantly overhead on the 2nd of December, 2004 it was not a day for river fishing. A howling nor'west wind was building, even at 9.00am, and would have made fly-fishing on an exposed stream impossible. As a result my friends and I decided to seek a sheltered shore on Lake Alexandrina, one with the wind on our backs. As I stood lake-side the fury of the storm whipped up huge whitecaps on the lake and hurled them towards distant shores. *I'm not venturing far from this sheltered edge*, I thought to myself, and moments later more encouragement to "stay put" slipped past — a fine looking trout in search of food. My brother, Les, and John Cornish stood nearby also peering into the lake. "That was a good fish," I remarked. The measure of their interest was soon displayed as they moved away and disappeared from sight over a grassy ridge and under some willows.

Where I stood it was quite swampy, soft and spongy underfoot — almost wobbly to stand on. The water, not more than a few centimetres from my feet, was probably three metres deep. I looked out into the lake edge through a narrow gap in some raupo. For ten or fifteen minutes I watched the sunlit bed, willing the fish to return. When it did re-emerge, nosing the bed, I was encouraged by its size — about three kilograms I estimated. As the fish slipped away I flicked a little dry onto the lake's surface, trying to encourage it to rise but it was not tempted. While it patrolled along the edge of the raupo (that's where I assume it went) I replaced the fly with a small nymph and waited once more, line coiled in my left hand ready to have the nymph airborne in an instant. Soon the opportunity arose and my nymph plopped ahead of the fish. This time it tipped up on its tail, just enough to show it had looked (and excite me enormously), then dropped its head and moved away.

As I mentioned, three metres of water separated the fish and me, so next I decided to try a weighted nymph — a little tungsten headed one that would sink in haste. Not the choice of a purist — a match-the-hatch type — I knew, but no one was watching! The next time the fish came into view I was able to drop the nymph with the fish facing me. The nymph plopped audibly and promptly began its descent. At the same moment the fish lifted from the bed. Nymph and trout met half way, the fish's jaws opened showing the white insides of its mouth, then they closed. I struck and clung to the butt of my rod with two hands. At an enormous rate I lost line — it whistled from my reel and moments later much of it, along with the fish erupted clear of the water. I can still picture the monstrous flanks high in the air. Suddenly aware of the true proportions of the fish I became immediately tense and apprehensive.

For the next fifteen or twenty minutes an uncompromising "tug of war" ensued. The fish would head out into the lake but luckily eventually slow and turn. Then I'd gradually coax it back to shore before its next bid for freedom.

I was battling the monster with a 1.8 kilogram tippet! This added to my anxiety enormously especially when the fish, after being encouraged back to shore for the fourth time, decided to dive headfirst into the raupo. It remained there quite immobile. I didn't know if it was just resting or had snagged the line. I clung to my rod and came as close as I ever have to praying.

It was during this inactive stage of the battle that a dilemma came to mind. I was alone. The others would never believe that I had landed a monster (if indeed I had that fortune). What should I do? The possibilities sped through my head. Just hold on with the fish swimming about until my mates arrived? Net the fish and click off a couple of quick pictures on my digital camera before releasing it? Try to attract their attention?

I began shouting. "LES, JOHN!" They did not reappear. The next call, and the one that followed had more urgency, a higher pitch and more prolonged — "LEES, JOOHN, LEEES, JOOOHN!"

Les and John were fishing in a more sheltered spot among the willows. hundreds of metres away, but fortunately they were downwind — and remember this was a good blow. They told me later that they heard the shouts and began moving my way but when the tone changed they had visions of me drowning and their pace increased. I was delighted to see the two of them racing into view. I didn't wait for them to get close before yelling about size of the fish that bent my rod so much. Their pace increased — faster than it had been when they suspected that I was in trouble!

By the time that they were at my side the fish had foolishly backed out of the raupo and was now "mooching" around on the lake bed close to shore. Very fortunately it did not attempt to run because it was at this time that I discovered that the line had jammed in my reel. I'd been anxious before but now the emotion was panic. My hands shook violently as I attempted to free the line. The more I tugged the tighter it seemed to get. There was plenty of advice from "the gallery." While my hands worked furiously on the reel I stepped sideways and overbalanced into the edge of three metres of water. My rod arm shot into the air and the other hand grabbed the nearest swampy vegetation saving me from full immersion. When I regained my feet the reel jam had gone. The fish "mooched" on.

"Want me to net it?" asked Les.

"Thanks."

"I'll just get a picture first."

I tried to smile, aware of the focussing, the refocussing, the exposure check, the composition considerations, the pre-exposure checklist of a pedantic photographer. I was also aware of the time I had already battled this fish on a straining tippet. I picked up the net and stepped closer to the lake. Les got the hint!

Manoeuvring a six kilogram trout in three metres of water to an awaiting net is a delicate operation. I swear that I did not breathe for prolonged periods each time the fish was close to being scooped. Les did not lift the fish clear of the water when it was eventually trapped head-first — he couldn't. Instead its bulk was dragged onto the grass and then with a closer grasp with two hands on the net handle he hoisted it — its broad tail sticking out the top of the net. My prize was handed to me. I don't remember what I said at that moment. The relief was so great it was probably unprintable!

There are many lessons that could be drawn from the capture of Ho's huge trout. Observations about an angler's demeanour when attached to a trophy fish would be among the more interesting I'm sure, however, in the present context the story highlights an important feature of the way that lake edge fish feed. In turn this affects the way that a still water stalker should approach his hunt.

River fish live in running water and usually food is carried to them. Generally trout seek a place in the stream where there is plenty of food, they hold in their lie and intercept food as it passes — they lift or drift sideways (about one metre) for each morsel. In contrast, still water (lake edge) trout have to move and seek their meal. Most still water trout command a territory, a beat that they patrol continually — one of considerable length (tens to hundreds of metres).

A lake edge trout cruising in search of food.

While Ho could not watch his fish cover its entire territory he imagined that it was about fifty metres long. He understood that the fish would pass where he stood repeatedly, so there was no need for him to actively seek the fish. Instead his stalk required his patience in waiting for the fish to come to him.

This foraging feeding behaviour of still water trout leads to another important difference from river stalking for a still water angler. River fish often feed from a lie. River stalkers frequently seek these lies and then endeavour to "pin-point" trout. In lakes, "lies" rarely exist (except at a stream mouth perhaps), instead there are *AREAS* that are more likely to possess trout — places that have greater attraction for fish. Usually they are zones that are richer in food but also they may possess cover (like weed beds) or be close to the security of deep water. Ho's fish occupied one of these areas — it patrolled in deep water along the edge of a thick stand of raupo, a haven for aquatic and terrestrial insects alike. Judging from the fish's size the food was most abundant!

Feeding Areas In Lakes

Lakes, like the rivers that feed them, are extremely varied. They vary in size, shape, depth and endless other ways. However, they do possess some common features, zones that can be identified from the shore, places that for one reason or other are more likely to hold trout. It would make sense for stalking anglers to focus more of their attention on these places.

In chapter 1 I outlined some of the features of stream beds and banks that contribute to poor trout habitat and the features of good habitat. Still water environments similarly vary in their allure for trout. Generally features that lead to a healthy river are the same that contribute to a good still water environment too.

Lake edges which are usually the most attractive for cruising trout are those that are stable, support abundant aquatic life and have vegetated shores. Open, featureless shores with loose sands that are continually churned by wind-generated waves usually support only small numbers of trout.

A lake edge comprising immoveable stones and boulders and a shore thickly vegetated with grass, scrub and mature trees. Both bed and shore would harbour abundant trout food.

Likely Feeding Areas

Stream Mouths

Probably the greatest attraction of the area around the junction of a river or stream with a lake is the fact that the stream will carry food into the lake edge. The trout present patrol and help themselves. Sometimes, like when there is a mayfly hatch in the stream, the food will be very abundant. I've observed trout in a situation like this actually leave their still water habitat and move up the stream to the source of the food — and then drift back to the lake when the hatch ceased.

The junction of a stream and a lake. This stream being vegetated to its edge and having a bed of coarse stones would most likely support many aquatic insects, a lot of which would eventually drift into the lake edge and thus be available to trout cruising there.

Streams are often cooler than the lakes they feed. In summer this can attract trout too. I can remember one particular situation where dozens of trout congregated close to a stream mouth. The lake, being relatively shallow had warmed to 21 degrees (Celsius) in the summer sun. Meanwhile the stream that fed the head of the lake, having tumbled hurriedly from lofty peaks, was much cooler. I didn't have to stalk far that day!

River Deltas

Because the waters of a river are slowed very abruptly when they meet a lake most of the sediment being carried, and certainly the coarse material, is deposited quickly. The usual result is that a delta is formed. Deltas often extend from the shore on either side of the junction. Generally the larger the river the more extensive the resulting delta. Because of this foraging trout may seek food some distance away from the actual mouth. A broad delta will usually support several trout.

Lake Outlets

Lake outlets (and the top sections of outlet streams) tend to be the reaches of waterways with the most stable beds. They are usually free from turbulent inflows and highly fluctuating conditions. This is generally a favourable environment for the growth of aquatic plants and associated fauna. Trout numbers tend to be higher around and in lake outlets preying on abundant food.

Drop-offs

The glacial lakes of the South Island are distinct from most other New Zealand lakes in their form. Because they were carved by huge glaciers they have very steep shores along much of their length with no shallow water at all. Most other lakes, however, do possess shallow margins before their bed falls away into deep water. Often the junction between shallow and deep water is quite abrupt with the bed sloping steeply — hence the name drop-off. Cruising trout are frequently found feeding close to the drop-off. Some will actually follow the line of the drop-off while others will swim over it and venture into shallower water. The drop-off probably has several attractions for trout. The close proximity of deep water is undoubtedly important (for security). In summer there would be a distinct difference in water temperature between the shallow water near the shore and the deep water beyond the drop-off. Trout have been observed to cross the drop-off frequently in response to temperature. Different light and other physical conditions exist on either side of a drop-off affecting the bed ecology. Where favourable conditions exist the change in depth will further attract trout to the area.

A lively trout that was cruising along the drop-off (the slope leading steeply from shallow water into deep water) has just been hooked on a surface fly.

Weed Beds

While weed beds provide cover which in itself attracts trout, they also nourish hosts of aquatic animals. Snails for example thrive in weed beds, foraging on them in abundance and trout in turn seek their share of the snails.

While some weed beds do have a column of water over them (and it may be possible to fish above) — most often stalking fishermen would search and fish the margins or consider channels cutting through.

The Margins Of Emergent Plants

Several years ago I fished with Len Cook on the shores of Lake Denny in Canterbury. I remember the occasion because while I stalked along a considerable length of shore and caught nothing, Len tarried beside an emergent weed bed and hooked several fish in a short time. Len could not see into the water particularly well so he just rested a dry fly about a metre off the weed bed and waited, watching all the time for his fly to be taken down. It was, several times! Len understood that trout frequently patrol along emergent beds (which are usually too dense for trout to weave through) feeding on aquatic life that may stray out of the bed or make its way onto the water nearby. His understanding and patience were rewarded. I was reminded!

Channels And Inlets

I particularly enjoy stalking the heads of lakes where most of the tributary streams flow in and broad deltas exist. In addition to the channel of the predominant feeder river or stream there are often several other channels — some carrying flowing water and others being stationary channels, the beds of previous streams. Whatever their form or origin, channels that link the deep water to the shore or even bite into the shore, offer a deeper passage for trout. And trout do use them. Any channel of deep water crossing lake shore shallows should receive some attention from stalking anglers who should watch for movement which is generally along the channel rather than across it.

Opposite page: An angler landing a trout that fed beneath the nearby beech trees. Note the underwater boulders which would create an environment that would support aquatic life (insects, snails, crustaceans and small fish). A fish cruising along this shore would have two sources of food – from above and below.

Under Overhanging Vegetation

Where trees or other tall vegetation hang out over a lake it is often difficult for fly fishermen to cast. However, I like places like this. Opportunist trout

that seek food that has "fallen" from leafy foliage usually cruise close to shore. Often a cast is not necessary, just some creative way of getting a fly onto the water coupled with a measure of angler concealment. I can remember vividly Brian Smith one day fishing the wooded edge of a small Canterbury lake. He was fishing, not from the shore, but from a precarious perch high in a beech tree. He was so high that his distance from the water offered some concealment. His "cast" was a vertical drop of a fly onto the water below. I watched from a nearby bank and wasn't surprised when he whipped the tip of his rod up to set the hook into a trout's jaw. Smithy wasn't surprised when I left him to land the fish! Angling with mates is a lot of fun!

Seasonal And Daily Patterns

Lake-edge stalking anglers can benefit a lot from understanding the areas of a lake where the majority of trout choose to feed. But they can also have more success through understanding some general daily or seasonal patterns or idiosyncrasies of a particular water. For example, smelt are a very important source of food for trout in the central North Island lakes. For most of the year the smelt remain offshore and trout feeding on them are not available to lake-edge anglers. However, in early summer (late November to January) smelt come into shallow water to shed their eggs and many trout follow them. At this time shore fishermen can have great sport.

Common bullies which are found in many New Zealand lakes also have a seasonal pattern of behaviour which can be targeted by shore anglers. Common bullies spawn in spring and early summer and the larvae move into the centre of a lake. However, in autumn maturing fish move closer to shore and become available to lake-edge cruising trout. Stalking anglers may profitably use a bully imitation late in a fishing season. During the middle of summer hosts of terrestrial insects make their way onto the surface of our lakes. Green beetles, cicadas and blow flies for example are gobbled in abundance by lake-edge trout (green beetles in December and January, cicadas in January and February and blowflies throughout summer) — and anglers using imitations of these large insects are usually pleasingly successful.

The pupal form of a midge is the stage of this insect's life cycle that is of most interest to anglers. As pupae rise to emerge they are vulnerable to preying trout. Emergence occurs most often early or late in a day — an activity that can be targeted by shore-bound fishermen. These are only a few examples of patterns that exist in lakes. Many general ones exist

A lake-edge stalker often has little time to present a fly to a trout that is moving quickly. This angler, with plenty of line already stripped from his reel and controlled in his right hand, is ready to cast immediately.

while some are specific to particular areas and times. Anglers who learn and understand the life cycles of trout food and the behavioural responses of the predator will be more successful stalkers.

Read The Conditions

Adverse conditions, like those experienced on the day described at the beginning of this chapter, really test an angler's stalking skills. On this occasion the very strong wind dictated not only where we could fish but also affected the manner of our approach. While Ho stood among shoulder high raupo, willing "his" fish to return, John Cornish and I sought an even more sheltered spot among some willows and behind a steep scrub-covered ridge. We soon found a gap in the trees, one wide enough to accommodate two anglers standing shoulder to shoulder.

Protected from the wind, the lake edge was surprisingly calm but a few metres out waves a metre high rolled along while those a little further out reached even greater heights and broke continually. We began a vigil of watching the calmer water, watching and waiting for a cruising fish to appear. The wind rippled the water's surface incessantly, however, a bright sun shone down and the lake bed showed reasonably clearly right out to the drop-off.

It is easier to spot trout cruising a lake shore when the bed is composed of light coloured material like white sand or pale rocks. Over a whitish bed a trout's dark dorsal side contrasts well or its dark shadow will show distinctly. However, whether the bed is light or dark toned, a trout cruising close to the surface will also show well when the sun is shining. We were battling a nasty wind but the sun shone nonetheless. In addition the wind came largely from behind, whipping through the grass, scrub and trees hurling debris onto the water. We reasoned that some terrestrial food should be part of the flotsam — drawing any watchful fish to the surface.

Within a short time the first of several trout cruised by — near to the drop-off, a short cast from the shore. It moved quickly, a rainbow of about two kilograms, sipping from the top frequently. We were caught unawares and by the time I'd stripped sufficient line from my reel to begin casting the fish was a safe distance away. But I was ready for the next.

In addition to using light coloured beds as "spotting boards" lake-edge stalkers can also seek tall opposing horizons to darken the backdrop and thus assist visibility into the water. High backdrops are much more frequent on narrower streams and rivers than on lake shores — but where they do exist they offer an advantage to anglers. Ahead we were faced by a broad expanse of water with a low horizon. However, we did enjoy the benefit of an elevated viewing position, another advantage which stalking anglers can seek.

When the next fish (shorter and dumpier) appeared and passed in haste I whipped my rod and a handful of line into the air in an instant and let the wind grab it and hurl it onto the water. The fish pounced onto my small green beetle and I struck in return. This was the first of two catches. While I battled the fish with two hands on my rod, I could no longer hold my hat down. Soon it flew from my head, landing in the water, ten metres distant. "Quick John," I bellowed, forgetting the fish momentarily, "cast out and grapple my hat!"

Three flicks later John and I had a double hook-up — me a 1.5 kilogram trout and John a battered and soiled, but much-loved hat. The fish provided the better fight.

Once the fish was netted and the tension eased from the line, my beetle imitation fell loose into the trout's jaw. However, it was interesting to note that two natural beetles also lay in the fish's gaping mouth — some of the flotsam that we suspected would be deposited by the wind. My choice of fly had been informed on this occasion — we were in green beetle country and December is the beginning of the time they emerge then fall.

Divert Occasionally

Most anglers who stalk their fish test their skill on rivers and streams. Usually I'm no different in this respect. However, the shallow edges of still waters are well worth exploration on occasions as well. Sometimes, when river conditions prevent fishing (like after heavy rain) a lake edge stalk may be the only fishing available or when a strong downstream wind blows the lee edge of a lake may provide the best opportunities for sight fishing. And sometimes, a lake edge may provide the most enjoyable sport, be the first choice for a stalk in ideal conditions. Lake edges can be spectacularly beautiful. On calm days reflections appear, colours are absorbed and intensified. Trout numbers can be quite high. The fish can suddenly appear and approach from one of several directions. They may feed amazingly close offering "nose to nose" fishing for a concealed angler.

Being deeper, still waters hide their secrets better than streams. They conceal a share of monster trout. They harbour feisty trout particularly when they're hooked in shallow water. They possess endless opportunities for a stalking angler who is prepared to be diverted their way at least occasionally.

PART 2 : Catching Trout

Preface To Part 2 : Another Mid-life Crisis?

In the late 1980s I finally decided to eschew the life of a country school teacher to become a full-time trout fishing guide. The catalyst was the construction of a luxury fishing lodge, to which I was able to offer my services, just minutes from my home at Ngatimoti in the idyllic Motueka Valley. By this time I had taught full-time for around twenty years, but more and more I felt that I was losing my enthusiasm for the career I had once loved so much. In my first season guiding I did only 30 days and supplemented my income by near full-time day to day and long term relief teaching, which I found very enjoyable on the whole, as it was possible to do the job and not become embroiled in internal politics as full-time staff inevitably did. For more than ten years I juggled the two jobs but towards the end of this time I was able to be quite choosy about the teaching assignments I accepted and gradually reduced my classroom time to a mere handful of days per year.

Fly fishing had long before become a passion with me, a love affair which I simply could not give up if I tried. In the course of evolving as an angler my skill level in such matters as spotting and making accurate casts increased in quantum leaps from the early, tentative, frustrating days when my clumsy approach and poor presentation simply resulted in clearing the water of potential targets. Slowly but surely though, my skills improved to a point where, weather and river conditions allowing, catching a few fish on any given outing was not too difficult.

Much of this success was founded on a steady increase in my level of confidence. Attitude is a topic to which sports psychologists give a great deal of lip service. Similarly, fly fishing successfully is a pastime which is implicitly linked to a positive mental state, and this is an aspect which will be dealt with in more detail elsewhere.

However, making the transition from active participant to guide and mentor is a massive step. Not only has one to attempt to place oneself in the shoes of the client but also provide advice on so many aspects, some of which have simply become second nature to the guide. At first it is very difficult to inform a man who may be an eminent surgeon or the chief executive of a multi-million dollar company that he is likely to scare every trout within 100 metres by wading up the stream so clumsily, or that he must not flail the water with every false cast.

I frequently found myself making comments like this.

"Yes, I know the cutthroats and dolly vardens out west don't mind but we are dealing with an entirely different branch of the family here. Old *salmo trutta* has eyes like a pronghorn antelope and is able to pick up vibrations in the water from miles away."

Guiding is about developing trust, not unlike school teaching. As soon as the client (or student) begins to suspect that the guide (or teacher) is unsure of his or her ground, doubts about that person's ability begin to surface, distrust prevails, with the potential to negate the strength of a good student to teacher relationship. Therefore guides need a quietly assertive manner without being over-bearing. Pontification and bluster do little to endear either a teacher or a guide. Regrettably, some who have chosen guiding as a career tend to be "know it all," personality types who inevitably find themselves involved in disputes with their clients. There is a major difference between assertiveness and dominance. For want of a better term I call these people "prima donnas," as some even behave like spoilt opera stars and indulge in little tantrums. I believe in leaving that kind of behaviour to the clients if they so choose, and a small minority do choose to.

It didn't take long to realise that turning one's favourite recreation into a job was no simple matter, and that if I was to be successful a great deal of hard work was required. Living in the Motueka Valley and working as a teacher had turned me into something of a "fair weather angler." If conditions were right I could pop out for the evening rise at any one of dozens of locations, some of which were situated less than five minutes drive from my gate. Similarly, conditions willing, I could spend a few hours on a Saturday or Sunday morning sight fishing for trout on the Motueka or one of its tributaries. Because conditions were invariably favourable during these outings success was nearly always guaranteed. Guiding is an entirely different situation. Clients are booked, sometimes more than a year ahead, for specific dates. Even if it's pouring down and all the rivers are in flood they expect to go fishing. In twelve or thirteen years I could probably count on the fingers of two hands or less the number of times when I had to inform the client that fishing that day was simply out of the question. Many's the time we fished on days which appeared impossible, and with some surprisingly good results. Sometimes it simply meant a long drive to another, less affected part of the region, concentrating on headwaters or working the mouths of small streams where they entered larger waters. The ability to think laterally and knowledge of a wide range of waters was imperative. I would like to think that it improved me as an angler too and that the experience gained was invaluable.

I wasn't even sure that I would enjoy guiding as a career. Indeed, initially at least, I saw the whole process as more like recreation than work. Sometimes it was pure, unadulterated fun with perfect weather, an affable, pleasant client and willing fish. At the other end of the spectrum was the stress associated with terrible weather, a morose or grumpy customer and difficult fish. A combination of all three is a recipe for sleepless nights and some of the highest stress levels I have experienced in any occupation. But I did take to guiding as I like being with people and getting to know them well, and I have always enjoyed seeing others experience success, especially if it is hard won and a just reward for diligence and effort.

I once recall a friend and well-known fishing guide state that he really knew very little about fly fishing until he took up the challenge of guiding for a living. While he may be over-stating the case to make a point there is certainly an element of truth in the contention, and I find myself now agreeing to some extent. I would go a step further though and add that the combination of many, many hours as an amateur and also as a professional have been responsible for a growth in knowledge and expertise. I would also like to think that the thousands of hours spent with clients have also made me a better teacher and mentor.

Chapter 6 : Preparing To Do Battle

One of the first clients I ever guided was arguably one of the most difficult I had to manage during a guiding career spanning more than a decade. Al (not his real name) was wealthy beyond my wildest dreams. On the day I arrived at the lodge to meet him for the first time he was busy on the phone finalising the purchase of a number of art works on which he had placed bids. He seemed very pleased with himself and it later transpired that he had spent upwards of $US100,000 to secure two works by an artist I had never heard of.

The trouble with Al was that he was not accustomed to being told what to do. A self-made man who had accumulated a fortune in a very competitive industry, he was often tetchy and irritable to a degree which required much tact, whilst maintaining the degree of assertiveness I alluded to in the preface. After a number of days in his company I realised that part of the reason for his irritability was directly related to the state of his health. He had survived a prostate cancer scare, but not long before leaving for his trip had been informed that the cancer had returned and would require further treatment. While initially somewhat overawed I realised that surviving seven days on the river with him was going to require a huge effort on my part. His angling skills were basic. While they may have been sufficient to fool tailwater rainbows or cutthroats the skill level was surprisingly low for someone who claimed to have fished for many years. This became a very familiar pattern indeed over the next dozen years or so as I learned to be very wary of those who claimed great expertise in the art of fly fishing. Almost without exception such people actually possessed a distinctly low level of prowess.

Al returned a number of times over the ensuing years as his cancer went into remission. He always insisted that I guide him even though we were barely on speaking terms by the end of each trip! He was not an easy person at the best of times. However, he kept coming back because once he had lifted his skill level he began to catch fish the like of which he could only dream of back in his native California. He never seemed to hold it against me that the atmosphere became decidedly icy as each trip wore on. I stood my ground and continued to analyse his technique whether he liked it or not, and I would like to think that we ended up friends, as he always greeted me as one at the start of each new trip. I suspect he would have had very little respect for me had I caved in and not insisted on modifications to his angling style.

The first fault I had to try and cure was a careless, clumsy approach to the river. He knew nothing of a trout's ability to detect vibrations through the streambed, and was quite incredulous when I deigned to mention that a trout has two hearing systems. Besides "ears" in the conventional sense it also possesses a lateral line via which it is able to pick up tiny vibrations. Initially he dismissed such a proposition as sheer hocus pocus. It almost seems elementary to make such a simple observation but many anglers are guilty of transgressing in this way. Trout are truly wild creatures which have evolved a remarkable ability to sense the presence of danger in its many forms. Superb sight, wonderful protective coloration and the ability to detect vibrations constitute a formidable suite of defence mechanisms.

Al was not one to admit to indiscretion. Consequently, it took much effort on my part to convince him that his bumblings were impacting heavily on his angling success. The message did finally get through, at least to a degree. He was never going to become a real Twinkletoes but as success came so too did a grudging acceptance of my advice.

Before we even stepped onto the river bank much work had to be done. On our very first outing on the Motueka my man proudly produced a highly expensive Abel reel to match his Sage rod. The only problem was that the line was coloured bright orange! Obviously the well meaning salesperson back in the States had equipped him as best he could, but with no understanding of his New Zealand quarry. Indeed, in those days most anglers came to fish our brown trout water with lines of many brilliant hues. While they were no impediment to success on many US waters they were a definite handicap in the South Island. I was not a popular chap but I stood firm on this one.

"Al, you use my reel and olive green line today and tonight I'll dye yours a sensible colour."

This was not the most auspicious start to the expedition and all day long I fielded complaints about not being able to see the line on the water and disparaging remarks about my "crappy" reel. I simply remained tight-lipped or made encouraging noises when he effected a useful cast or made a good mend. Gradually the protests lessened and eventually ceased altogether as a form of truce prevailed. I would like to think that the reasons for use of dull, natural-hued lines are obvious. On a bright day line flash and also that from chromed rod rings, reel seat and even the face of the reel are all dead giveaways to wary fish. We have seen fish flee as soon as line is lifted off the water on so many occasions as to be totally convinced of the need to avoid reflection off shiny surfaces wherever possible. I'll even go so far as to run the leader and tippet through a handful of sand to remove some of the glint.

It turned out that Al had an arsenal of equipment — rods of various makes and reels to match. Fortunately he had the gear for most contingencies as we explored a great range of water types and had to battle the elements which definitely conspired against us, especially on the very first trip. In fact we only encountered one delightfully good, clear day after a major rainstorm. But on this day, towards the end of his trip the fishing finally lived up to its much vaunted reputation. After helicoptering into a remote backcountry river Al took one beauty of just under 4kg and a number of other notable fish. It was one of the few times I saw him smile and I still have the photograph to prove it.

I recall the very first day on the Motueka vividly, partly because I lost my brand new weigh net as we made a somewhat difficult crossing right at the end of the day. We were almost fishless, as only two fish came to the net, and one of those was best described as a "tiddler." Despite it being the middle of February the day was grey and an unseasonably cool southerly made for near impossible spotting conditions and difficult casting for one whose expertise in this field was suspect at best. After straining my eyes to the maximum for an hour or two I knew that success would only come if we targeted high probability water by fishing blind. My man had been encouraged by his agent to undertake this trip with promises of fishing to large, clearly visible fish and was not keen on the seemingly random approach, but I insisted firmly and very nearly despaired when I realised just what I was dealing with. Almost every false cast slapped the water, no attempt was made to mend line, and he was hopelessly out of touch with his indicator as the line drifted in huge bellies back towards him. Catching an "educated" Motueka brown would be something of a minor miracle.

It was "back to basics" time. I decided on something I very, very rarely do — to demonstrate — but demonstrate I did. After flailing the water for half an hour he was only too happy to take a breather. I tried to impress on him that each cast should be made with conviction — with real commitment to a hook-up. To his credit Al listened and observed. People don't become multi-millionaires by totally ignoring good advice. Despite his crustiness he could appreciate that there was some merit in the demonstration. I was just handing the rod back when I noticed a rise towards the top end of the long run we were on. There it was again — the

unmistakable and very welcome sight of a really nice fish lifting boldly to take something riding the surface. I had not been aware of a mayfly hatch — just the odd mayfly dun so common to this river, but both sides of the river were clothed in manuka and beetle patterns had worked well for me in this vicinity before. Even though it was a bit late in the season for the green manuka beetle I decided that an artificial was worth a try.

I have rarely felt as nervous as I did right then as I dispensed with the nymph rig and tied on a #12 Green Humpy. I had originally considered a Coch y Bondhu, as good a beetle pattern as any, but with the downside of being very difficult to see on the water in poor light. First I had to get Al into position as I really wanted this fish to take. Urging the utmost care not to bang the cobblestone size rocks together we slowly edged up to within casting distance. I anxiously scanned the area where I had observed the last rise, hardly daring to breathe and praying that the fish would remain in position long enough for a good shot at it. Yes, there it was again, off to the side a bit but still in the vicinity. I judged that the fish was content to feed in the relative confines of a substantial pocket. Even though no rocks protruded through the surface I knew from many previous times on this stretch that the mainly cobblestone sized rocks were interspersed with occasional much larger ones, turning relatively featureless water into

108

a place with excellent cover and streambed stability, an area which had produced many very good fish for me over the preceding years.

Again, urging the utmost caution we made our way at a virtual snail's pace along the bouldery bank to a point where I judged we could enter the water. There was no close natural cover here and I feared all the time that the fish would become aware of us in such an exposed location. The still rather stiff south-westerly actually did us a favour by ruffling the water surface to some degree. Fixing my gaze on the trout's feeding area we finally made it to my pre-determined entry point. Taking a firm grip of his left elbow I eased my client out into the current. The fish continued to feed some four or five metres from our bank. The breeze was a worry. While not as strong as during the earlier part of the day it was still mainly in our faces but blowing more across than directly downstream. I knew that this would necessitate moving into a position directly downstream of or even slightly further out in the current than where the fish was located, as I suspected that my client would have little chance of punching a decent line directly into the wind.

It seemed to take ages to reach the spot but soon we were stationed in knee-deep water a little to the right of the obligingly hungry fish. The wind gusted in from our right but was not constant now and occasionally almost ceased. Line shadow, whilst normally a consideration, especially early in the day was not a problem in the largely overcast conditions. Ensuring that Al had a good, firm stance I proceeded to explain the plan to him. First though I examined the fly and leader, checking carefully for "wind", or more correctly "casting" knots and then had him strip a few metres of line

An angler with floating line drifting behind in the current – enough to begin loading the rod immediately the line is lifted into the air. This gives the angler immediate control of the fly.

An angler stripping several metres of line out before beginning to cast to an upstream fish.

off the reel and allow the fly to drift down the current.

I suspected that my client still had not seen a rise form and was probably not going to. If he was to effect a hook-up I would need to call the strike, another factor adding to the general stress I was feeling right then. The next step was to attempt to direct the cast in the right direction — easier said than done as we were on a long, wide and relatively featureless run. However, a line of stately Lombardy poplars, a real feature of the Motueka stood proudly erect across the river on the true left bank and it was easy to identify one to be aimed at. Assessing distance was not quite so easy but this time I pinpointed a clump of dead gorse lying uprooted on the near shore and indicated that this was about as far up as the cast should go.

The last aspect to be considered was the line of the current and to ascertain if any compensation would be required to achieve a dead drift as much as possible. The trout was feeding about ten metres downstream of a very distinct shallow rapid which angled diagonally across the river towards the furthest upstream poplar on the far bank. By the time the current reached the fish's feeding position though it had virtually straightened into a laminar flow. I could foresee no major problem with drag in this situation and chose not to even mention mending so as not to confuse the situation.

I was so concerned about spooking the fish that I stressed the importance of making a really good first cast. To try to ensure that he had the correct length of line out I suggested that Al try a few false casts directly out into the river to the side of our position, insisting that the line be kept off the water at all times whilst false casting. Despite the breeze he managed this pretty well. The moment of truth had arrived. Perhaps it was because it was so early in my guiding career that I felt incredibly nervous about the outcome and wondered if such trepidation would ease as I gained more experience. For some strange reason there were times when I was afflicted with the same malaise many years and hundreds of days guiding later. It reminded me a lot of the apprehension I used to feel as I stepped up to the starting line in my middle distance running days.

Once again I ensured that Al knew exactly where I wanted the fly to land and uttered words of encouragement whilst trying desperately to conceal my nervousness. Subsequently, but not before some anxious moments and a number of forgettable attempts which should have put the fish off its dinner Al did hook and land that fish, and a good one at that. But that's another story.

Preparation cannot be stressed enough. It is well worth while taking time to critically examine each new situation as it arises rather than rushing in and spoiling the opportunity. On numerous occasions I've been guilty of doing just that in my enthusiasm, convinced that the fish would depart if a cast was not made instantly. There certainly are times when swift action is required, particularly if the fish is moving around a pool or back-water, but the exercise of a little patience here may pay dividends too as it's likely that the trout is simply working a set beat. This is almost certainly the case in lakes and large backwaters, and even in pools in backcountry rivers where feeding fish constantly patrol their domain. Observation and planning of strategy can tip the balance in the direction of the angler.

Factors to consider include the angle of the sun, much more critical early in the day than later, in my experience. One section of the upper Karamea I have fished extensively was a case in point. Until late morning, even in mid-summer just a hint of line shadow was sufficient to scare any fish encountered, so the approach and line of cast had to be planned carefully.

I have long been a believer in positioning oneself as much as possible

An angler using cover while preparing to cast.

in direct line astern of a feeding fish and casting up along that line, laying out the leader and tippet over or just to the side of the fish. While this is a perfectly sensible strategy in many cases, it can be fraught with problems, especially where line shadow is an issue where the fish may have received a considerable amount of attention from other anglers. There are times when a cast up on an angle ranging from 20–45 degrees or even more may be more effective and less likely to result in either line shadow or the knife-like effect of the leader cutting the surface directly over the fish. On rare occasions a cast may need to be made from a concealed position upstream of the fish so that the trout sees the fly before it sees the tippet. Such measures may seem extreme but are very much in vogue on many of the famous spring creeks in the US, such as Silver Creek in Idaho where the upstream approach is virtually pointless with even the finest tippet and smallest fly.

Whilst there are occasions when I actually prefer to fish alone and just lose myself in my personal thoughts it is much more fun and usually more productive to share the experience with a companion. It never ceases to amaze me how much more a well concealed fishing friend or guide can see from different locations.

Just this summer I had the pleasure of guiding two wonderful Englishmen for a few days on Westland's Grey and some of its tributaries. The weather was hot and dry, in fact simply too hot some days as we just wilted during the mid-afternoon hours, especially whilst traversing the large, white granite boulders which typify a lot of this water. Late one morning things were just a little slow with only a few smaller fish cooperating. Intermittent cloud and a stiff breeze made spotting quite difficult and a careful stalk all the way up one very nice looking run produced a total blank. With all the skill I could muster my sight fishing efforts were futile. The far bank was clothed in the typical mix of manuka and beech forest with a dense understorey of bushy shrubs, and convinced that the run held fish I elected to retrace my steps a hundred metres back downstream, cross over and make my way up along the high bank through the dense vegetation. What a difference a bit of elevation made! Carefully parting the greenery at strategic intervals I peered down into the clear water. From here every rock was visible but it wasn't until I was about twenty metres from the top of the run that I spied a fish, and a beauty at that. From my concealed position I could just about count every spot. It held position just

Two anglers fishing together. The angler on the bank (particularly if in an elevated position) can usually see more of what is happening in the water than the angler below. The spotter on the bank must keep a low, concealed profile.

An angler using cover while casting to a fish.

An angler keeping a low profile while surveying ahead. He would be paying particular attention to the froth line showing on the true right shore and pushing out into the stomach of the pool.

30 or 40 centimetres from the bank and periodically swung out into the current to intercept (to me) unseen food items in the drift. Just as I was about to call Hugh over I glanced upstream and was thrilled to see another, similar-sized fish just ahead. If this wasn't enough a bit more observation revealed three more for a total of five, and yet not one had been even remotely visible from the other bank. The "boys" subsequently hooked three of the five. I must confess that unfortunately none were landed. This incident proved the worth of using the skills of a well concealed companion and was to prove its value on a number of other occasions that day.

Whilst definitely more difficult when fishing alone the same technique of using cover and elevation can produce results. The critical factor here is marking the exact location of the fish so that the spot can be pinpointed from down at water level even if the fish itself cannot be seen. While this may seem elementary, in practice it is sometimes far from being so, requiring excellent powers of observation so the cast can be made with complete confidence to the correct position.

At all times a stealthy, quiet approach is mandatory. Keeping a low profile, even crawling and ensuring that the rod is pointed to the rear are simple but effective means of remaining undetected.

Two anglers working together. The more elevated spotter is standing behind the angler and back from the water's edge.

Too often anglers ignore some relatively simple aspects and like the proverbial fools, rush in. Once the optimal casting position has been reached a careful survey of the prevailing wind direction and a good, close look at the current is essential. Try to ascertain if compensation for wind is needed. Sometimes a much exaggerated cast to one side is the only way that the fly is going to get within the fish's feeding and visibility zone. One needs to try to judge what the current will do once the floating fly line is on the water. Unnatural drag more than any other single factor may make the difference between success and failure. If it appears that drag will greatly affect the drift of the fly then it is likely that a cast which places the fly very close to the fish will be necessary. Conversely, if using terminal tackle in the form of a double nymph rig the cast should be made in order that the nymphs enter the water well ahead of the fish so it is not alerted by the splash and allowing time for the flies to reach the depth at which feeding is taking place. Again though, I cannot stress the importance of observation, correct preparation and a positive mental attitude.

Chapter 7 : Into The Fray

"Right. Al, you are going to catch this fish," I stated with all the confidence I could muster.

"D'ya reckon I can Graeme?"

"Yep. Not a problem," I replied, lying like a trooper, as I had serious reservations despite our meticulous efforts thus far.

"For all I know you might just be pulling my leg. I can't see any fish rising. Why out west there'll be dozens of 'em all coming up at the same time."

"Yeah, and the biggest of them would be 15 inches long," I replied callously. "This is a good fish Al, a Kiwi brown trout, not one of your sardines."

I returned my gaze to the still rising fish, somewhat puzzled by the lack of obvious food drifting down. However, I wasn't going to complain as it was clearly targeting something of interest. Quickly I explained again just where I wanted the cast to land, making sure there was no confusion over which markers I was referring to.

"OK Al, go for it."

The floating line lay stretched out on the water behind us.

"Strip a bit in Al," I suggested. "It'll make it easier to pick it up off the water."

An angler "on point." A trout has been spotted upstream and the angler has positioned himself downstream and is about to prepare to cast.

An angler with his line drawn downstream behind him. With the line out straight like this he has a good platform from which to lift into his next cast.

He did as I suggested and after easing the grip of the surface tension of the water was able to lift the line into the air in a fairly respectable forward cast.

"Keep it up off the water," I commanded urgently as I sensed that the whole line was perilously close to slapping the water in front of us.

"OK, let a bit more out and put it down — gently."

My personal stress level was building unbearably but he was making a tolerable job of it and the wind wasn't too much of an impediment. The line snaked out and landed, a little more heavily than I would have preferred but not too badly. However, it placed the fly a metre or so behind the position of the fish's last rise and off to the left.

"Right, this time get a bit more line out and fix on a point about two metres further up. Aim a little more to the right. The breeze took it too far left that time."

I winced as the floater almost touched the water on the false cast again and I hardly dared breathe. This time the fly line went away off to the right as the angler over-compensated. This pattern continued for a number of attempts and it seemed that he was simply unable to make the necessary adjustment. But finally the leader was laid out right along the path I wanted.

An angler in the best position to cast to the fish ahead. The vegetation on the bank would prevent the sometimes preferred angled cast from the right while wading further to the left would involve excessive movement and risk detection by sound.

An angler applying downstream sidestrain, pivoting his fish towards the shore.

"Get ready, ready, wait — Go!" I screamed as the fish came up and sucked in the fly with total confidence. My client heaved back, lifting the rod tip high and almost fell over in the process. As the fish felt the hook it panicked and the water boiled. We had made contact.

"Let it run," I yelled and reached forward ready to prise his fingers from the reel handle as the rod tip bent alarmingly. Fortunately he reacted swiftly enough and the reel played its sweet music. It may have been a "crappy" reel by Al's standards but it worked just fine as line peeled off smoothly. In typical Motueka brown trout fashion the first long run was made diagonally up and across the broad stretch.

"Let go," I barked. "Don't try to stop it or it'll bust you for sure."

"Wow, some fish Graeme. I just can't stop it."

"Just don't even try," I retorted. Be patient and we'll get it."

Something of an impasse developed as the fish sought sanctuary in the shallows on the far side of the river. The initial run had taken out the

An angler applying downstream sidestrain on a fish pressuring it towards the shore.

entire fly line and at least twenty or thirty metres of backing before the brown almost beached itself on the true left shore.

"OK Al, we're going to apply some sidestrain. Point the rod tip downstream and hold the rod parallel to the water. Now start walking down the run. Keep firm contact and the fish should start to come across."

The gradual pressure and the sheer weight of line started to tell and slowly but surely the fish began to come across the current to our side. I breathed a sigh of relief as first all the backing and then part of the fly line came back onto the reel.

"Right, we're going to get you on the bank Al. Make sure you keep the slack out of the line."

Slowly, with me supporting and giving encouragement we backed off over the algae-coated cobblestones until we were on the rocky shore. The fish appeared to be coming in reasonably easily but with about 20 metres of line out it felt the gravel and stones under its belly, sensed that all was not well and gave three heart-stopping jumps clear of the water.

"Wow, look at that thing. It looks like a darned submarine," Al shouted as for the first time he became aware of the true size of the fish that he had a direct connection to.

"Browns don't jump," he yelled excitedly.

"Nobody told these ones that," I grinned.

A number of other panicked runs and a few more jumps followed but each became less energetic as the power of the well flexed rod took its toll.

"Keep the sidestrain on," I urged. "Keep walking it downstream. That keeps it off balance."

To his credit Al did exactly as asked. This fish was very important to him. That much was obvious. If I'd been nervous earlier it was nothing compared to the way I felt now with the fish so close yet still so far away. I knew that one false move here could wreck things completely. Trying to sound calm I urged my client to "walk" the fish into the shallows by backing off up the bank. In my experience even a large fish will come in quite easily by applying this method which simply involves a smooth drawing of the fish inshore whilst its head is pointing towards the bank and giving line when it is pointed back out into the current. So often the last panicking dash from the shallows is the one which breaks the tippet or pulls the fly from the fish's jaw.

On this occasion I stood downstream a little, urging Al to guide the fish towards me. Again, clumsy netting attempts are often the cause of lost fish, a thought which was very much in my mind at this time so I continued to offer advice as calmly and concisely as I could. The gallant fish made numerous attempts to regain the sanctuary of the fast, midstream current but eventually the constant pressure took its toll and Al was able to guide it around a large rock and into my waiting net head first. The relief was unbelievable. Anyone who considers guiding a stress-free vocation should think again. My hands were shaking almost uncontrollably as I hoisted the Mclean weigh net aloft.

Two anglers working together bringing a fish to the net. The angler playing the fish has backed away from the river and is easing the fish towards the bank. The netter awaits slightly downstream.

"Wow, just look at that thing," Al exclaimed."What a beauty! My God, it's the biggest trout I've ever caught."

The strength in the old man's handshake really surprised me as the bones in my right hand were almost broken in the spontaneous gesture. According to the scale in the net the nicely conditioned hen weighed in at just a few old-fashioned ounces under five pounds, a very good fish anywhere, and well above the average for the river. Why it had been rising alone and just what it had been targeting remains a mystery as the fish was soon released to fight other battles once the mandatory "grip and grin" photographs were completed.

The rest of the day was something of an anti-climax. We actually found a few more nice fish and I exhorted Al to continue fishing blind but his heart was never really in it and he fished with little commitment or conviction, a recipe for near certain failure. We had one really interesting encounter later in the day which a better angler would have capitalised on. I found a fish of similar size to the one he had caught feeding off the surface in a tiny back eddy which had formed downstream of a rocky bank extension. I knew this spot well and had frequently found fish there before. The back eddy could only be approached by walking up a gravel bar which split the main flow of the river. At least 80% of the river flowed by on

122

one side of the bar and the remaining 20% or less was funnelled down a narrow channel up to a metre or so in depth. When a good hatch was on there were often up to five or six sizeable fish to be found feeding right in the fast water in this channel and another in the aforementioned back eddy. The difficulty with this place was that a short cast directly across the current was the only way to target the fish in the eddy. The dreaded drag came into play almost instantly. I had enjoyed success on a few previous occasions though by placing the fly right on the fish's nose, making a small, smart mend and holding the rod high to keep as much line off the water as possible. For some odd reason, even though the casting position was directly across from the fish it was rarely alarmed by the presence of an angler and repeated casts didn't seem to bother it, something I've observed on many other occasions when a fish is up and feeding right in the film. It appears that the cone of vision is greatly reduced close up under the surface, and also explains why a fly has to land right on the fish's nose when fishing to rises in the twilight.

A trout being netted head first.

This day, try as he might, Al just couldn't get it together and the fly kept getting whipped away from the fish. After some thirty or forty minutes of this it finally tired of the game and slunk off into the sanctuary of some overhanging willows downstream. By then it was time to head back to the car as we had an hour's drive back to the lodge. It was whilst crossing back to the true right bank that the bungee cord on my landing net came adrift and the net disappeared never to be seen again despite a lengthy search. B----r, or words to that effect! Still, I had a reasonably happy client with his best trout to date recorded on film for posterity.

Novice anglers frequently experience all kinds of difficulty with line control, both in the air and on the water. To anyone starting out in fly fishing I would urge the taking of some expert advice by enrolling in a reputable fly fishing course. I certainly wish I had, as being largely self-taught tends to ingrain bad habits, some of which I would like to abstain from. While it is difficult to learn casting from a book the basics may still be learned this way. Possibly one of the best illustrations of good casting technique I've seen is depicted in well-known Christchurch angler, Chappie Chapman's book, *Dancing Rivers* published by Halcyon in 2003. Chappie is a master fly caster who makes it all seem very simple indeed. To achieve a skill level even a number of steps down the scale from his degree of proficiency would require a good coach, commitment and many, many hours of time spent on the water in all sorts of conditions. However, even "lesser mortals" can and do achieve a level of competency which is perfectly adequate for most situations. In reality most trout are caught within 10 metres of the angler, and frequently somewhat closer than that. But the ability to handle a strong downstream wind, slip a fly up under an overhanging branch or roll cast with a high backdrop in the rear are typical of skills which can make all the difference between success or failure. The adage that practice makes perfect is very apt and the best form of practice is out on the water where the prospect of actually catching something adds a bit of incentive.

Even average casters, like me, can obtain some satisfaction by concentrating on a number of key elements. The first is to always strip a reasonable amount of line from the reel before even attempting to cast. In the region of four metres, and allowing it to float downstream creates a good platform for getting the line in the air. Avoid false casts onto the water anywhere near where a fish is located. Always strive for a tight casting loop, something which is only achieved if sufficient line speed is applied and

Three stages of a full roll cast. A very useful skill to use particularly when there is a high obstruction behind. Often a partial roll cast can be executed by lifting the rod and some line (not waiting for the line to drop behind the shoulder as in the drawing) and then driving the rod tip forward. This will roll the line out and lift it from the water and provide a quick and sound platform for the next overhead cast.

always ensure that the rod comes to a complete stop at the end of the back cast. Like Chappie Chapman I say, "bollocks" to the old system of casting to the positions on a clock face. The length of line required and presence of wind either upstream or down will dictate just how far back on the back cast the rod should be allowed to go. Newcomers do often make the mistake of taking the rod too far back without sufficient speed to load it up and fail to apply the absolutely vital "stop". Get into the habit of looking over your shoulder to see just what the line is doing on the back cast and before long the loading will take place naturally, and you will feel when the optimum moment has occurred to begin the forward cast.

In the United States casting instructors place great emphasis on the ability to roll cast proficiently. This is a skill which has many applications in this country too. Sometimes the proximity of vegetation or a high bank precludes a normal cast making the roll technique invaluable. I frequently use a partial version of it too in order to lift line off the water. Perhaps one of the situations where it can really make a difference is whilst engaged in close range blind nymphing. Here, roll casts avoid the wastage of valuable time with line swishing backwards and forwards in the air. Try practising in different types of water to develop consistency and fluency.

We live in a very breezy environment no matter what part of the country we inhabit. Whilst some wind, especially a light to moderate up-stream one can provide great assistance to casting, too much can be a severe

A cast being made out to the side of a a fish (well away) to gauge line length.

An angler with his line in the air, mentally and visually measuring line length and stripping more out during false casts as necessary.

impediment. I heartily dislike much more than a downstream zephyr, and of all the conditions one can encounter strong gusts from this direction will have me scurrying for the comforts of home quicker than any other, bar a tornado or severe electrical storm. It is well nigh impossible to cast effectively into a Canterbury 'norwester, though I know anglers who will persevere in their masochism. Some downstream winds are not constant and occasionally provide a brief lull which can be capitalised on. Otherwise the only coping mechanisms I know involve shortening the leader and shooting the line as low across the water as possible, where air velocity is always a little less close to the surface due to the effects of friction. Altering the casting angle can also assist. Double hauling on a short line to increase line speed can also work, but this is a specialised technique for already capable casters.

I have met some very fine anglers, some whose casting ability in windy conditions is astonishing, but none more so than my former guiding colleague and old friend Zane Mirfin. I recall one trip we did inland from Hanmer Springs one summer when the north-west wind blew constantly for the whole three days. We both caught some excellent fish with at least one each approaching the magic 4.5kg (10lb) figure, but where I struggled constantly Zane was able to extend line at least a few rod lengths upstream and consequently enjoyed the most success. The secret to his success was line speed which was aided considerably by the powerful Sage rod he was using. Quality equipment will also provide an edge. One of the top brand rods and a quality line which is cleaned frequently will greatly assist casting into the wind. Soft rods have their place but its definitely not out on a braided riverbed when the föhn wind is lifting clouds of dust into the air. If you are not a power caster then concentrate on other aspects. In many situations accuracy and an ability to control the line on the water are much more important than throwing out an entire floating line. We frequently allude to the importance of the first cast. The ability to place the fly right in the critical zone first time cannot be underestimated, as each successive cast has the potential to alert the quarry. Achieving accuracy goes hand in hand with the ability to judge line length. With experience one achieves this almost instinctively, but casts out to the side can help provide a gauge of distance.

If in doubt err on the side of caution by dropping the first cast short and then strip out the length required to cover the fish correctly on the next one. Practising on grass or a pond on a regular basis soon helps develop a feel for accurate casting and gives the confidence a major boost when faced with a feeding fish. Tie a piece of coloured wool to the tippet and place markers at measured distances to aim at. When you can consistently lay the leader out to within 20 or 30 centimetres either side of the marker you are probably casting accurately enough to encourage a take from a fish.

An upstream belly is forming in the line (the flow is right to left). A downstream mend would remove the loop and allow a longer drag-free drift of the fly.

Effective line mending, or the removal of unwanted loops of line from the water caused by variable flow, is an essential skill and one which makes all the difference at times. The upstream stalking approach which we advocate in the main relies upon being able to achieve a natural drift

127

past the fish which is as much as possible natural, and at precisely or very near the same speed as the current. Most trout, and especially browns, will rarely take either a fly or nymph which moves at a speed markedly divergent from the current speed, or is inclined to make an unnatural movement laterally or vertically. There are times when a trout will be induced to take a nymph moving quickly upwards through the water column as in the case of a nymph rising into the surface film. Indeed, the famous Leisenring lift induced take technique advocates accentuating this movement. In the main we advocate a dead drift technique whether fishing nymph or dry fly, especially the latter (with the notable exception of caddis (sedge) in the twilight.)

Line on the water is instantly influenced by the current so it is imperative that line be stripped in towards the angler once the cast has been made at as near as possible the speed which gives the fly a truly natural appearance to the trout. A cast made even a little off the line of directly upstream will soon be under the influence of the current and a belly will begin to form. Too many anglers fail to appreciate the effect this is having on the speed of the fly, especially if there is an area of calmer water between the angler and the position of the fish — a very common situation when fishing the eye of a pool or run. Unless the angler intervenes and applies

A solid strike using both a lift of the rod tip and a grip on the line with the left hand. The chances are high that the fish will run moments after being hooked so the angler should be prepared to let line move freely through the left hand and ease the rod tip forward to let the line run.

remedial action by mending, the fly will soon be accelerated to point where it may not just be of little interest to a fish but may actually cause it to become alarmed so that it quickly departs for a safer place.

Effective mending is an art that can be learned quite quickly. To me the key is to begin the mending process almost immediately a cast has been made and in most cases use just enough movement of the rod to move the fly line without moving the fly. This is not always easy but one becomes more proficient with time and experience. Sometimes just one or two large mends involving a deliberate lift of the rod arm will suffice but the direct opposite is also true at times, requiring tiny flicks or rolling of the rod tip with nothing more than short, sharp wrist movements.

If your mends are causing the fly to move then cease as no mending is better than a mend which creates a dragging fly. Mending is particularly important when fishing blind and should be synchronised with the rod tip pointing towards the fly. One has to try to visualise where fish might be lying and then drift the fly to that position. When fishing with nymphs mending assists them to get down towards the bottom where the fish are most likely to be feeding by slowing down the fly line and leader.

In recent years we have been somewhat bemused by the incredible amount of time and space in fly fishing magazines dedicated to the process of striking, so let's examine in some detail just what happens when a trout takes in an item of food.

Kurt D. Fausch in his excellent article in the winter 1992 issue of *Trout* magazine, *Trout As Predator* breaks the feeding sequence down into its component parts. He describes these stages thus:

1. Detection
2. Approach
3. Fixation
4. Inspection
5. Attack
6. Manipulation and Ingestion
7. Rejection (of unpalatable prey, for example, an artificial fly)
8. Return to the focal point.

Perhaps the stages in this sequence of most interest to us as predators of trout are 5, 6 and 7. Fausch couches his language in scientifically accurate terminology but for the lay person he explains that a trout attacks its prey by swimming towards it in a burst, followed by a rapidly occurring sequence involving opening of the jaws, gill covers and the membranes that enclose the gills on the bottom of the jaw. These actions result in rapid suction of the prey into the mouth. The fish then closes its mouth, opens the gill covers and squeezes the mouth and throat region thereby forcing water out of the throat and past the gills and gill rakers. These latter are designed to prevent prey from escaping. Larger prey, for example, small fish, are actually bitten, spat out and eaten again.

As any experienced trout fisher knows though, the rejection of unpalatable food such as an artificial fly which occurs with the re-opening of the mouth can be amazingly swift. Trout become very discriminating in this regard. Consequently trout rarely hook themselves. It behoves the angler to actually "set" the hook while the mouth is closed. I find it interesting that trout very rarely ever swallow an artificial fly. Indeed the vast majority of fish are hooked in the jaw region or in the upper or lower mouth interior. Hook-ups on the exterior surfaces are not uncommon, perhaps indicating that the fish simply missed ingesting the fly or else that it was hooked as the fly was pulled from the fish's mouth in the act of striking.

Timing remains one of those contentious issues which anglers everywhere will argue about forever. One school of thought is that a nymph strike should always be swift by comparison with the dry fly. I do not necessarily agree, contending that the speed of the water being fished is perhaps the most critical factor. On the whole though, if relying on an indicator to signal the take I would certainly recommend not wasting time. If the indicator stops, dips or appears to move upstream the fish has certainly taken the nymph into its mouth and the angler should react accordingly. However, it is possible to strike too soon and with too much violence, resulting in what many guides refer to as "ripping" with the result that the hook is pulled violently from the mouth or the tippet parts company with the nymph which is left firmly embedded in the fish's jaw.

I have known times when even in quite swiftly moving water the fish were taking nymphs in a relatively leisurely fashion necessitating just a simple turn of the wrist and a gentle lift to achieve a hook-up. I recall this happening to me on the Motueka River one glorious February day when I missed fish after fish by striking too soon and too swiftly. In desperation I resorted to the opposite tactic with immediate success including the capture of one of my best ever fish from that river.

The dry fly strike is the one which really instigates strong opinions and vigorous debate. I have been on some rivers on days when the takes on surface artificials were so swift that it was difficult to react quickly enough. In the main these lightning swift takes tend to come from smaller (less than one kilogram) fish and in very fast water where they have to be quick or else face the prospect of missing out on a meal. The speed of rejection is the astonishing thing, for if the fly is considered unpalatable it is rejected swiftly despite Fausch's lengthy list of the actions which must occur.

To me the debate over the speed at which one strikes when a dry fly is taken by a trout boils down to one crucial issue and that is simply if the fish has turned down or not, for even though it may have appeared to close its jaws on the artificial there is still a high chance of pulling the fly from the mouth by striking too soon. At times the angler must simply try to judge the precise moment at which the fish turns down — not an easy task in poor light or in joggly water. If the fish has turned down again there is a very good chance that setting the hook will result in it taking hold, hopefully firmly. Larger fish are often missed, because in the excitement of the moment the strike was just a little premature. Holding back just long enough for the fish to eject part of the water which it sucked in with the fly increases the odds for the angler.

Every angler will experience inexplicable misses when the timing appeared to be perfect. I suspect that heavily hackled dry flies may be part of the problem here. The stiff hackles which give the fly such great floatability also have a defect in that they push the hook itself away from somewhere to lodge.

Rise forms vary greatly depending on the type of surface prey being taken or even the stage in the insect's life cycle. The unhurried, sipping take of a mayfly dun contrasts with the "porpoising" action of a fish taking caddis off the surface. These latter fish are often amongst the easiest to hook as they literally roll over the top of the fly and take it down under the surface. Fish taking large terrestrials like cicadas often leave all caution behind and slash at the fly or else lift part of their heads above the surface in their eagerness. Each situation has to be judged on its merits. Observation is the key.

The debate over barbed versus barbless hooks also rages in angling circles. Whilst I don't believe that one style has superior penetration and holding ability over the other I will incur the wrath of many by contending that I have no particular preference for humane reasons. The keys to trout survival following capture are firstly getting it to the net as quickly as possible by using effective playing techniques and tippets which are as strong as practicable, and secondly not removing the fish from the water except for the briefest of periods once in the net. Unless a photograph is really desired I much prefer to see fish stay in the water. Always use forceps to remove the hook swiftly. I do not believe that a barbed hook causes significantly more damage or lessens a trout's survival chances than if a barbless hook were used. A barbed hook certainly leaves behind a larger mark where it penetrates but I doubt very much that this is likely to impact on a fish's longevity. The prime reason for using barbless hooks is the ease with which they may be removed. Most experienced anglers will at some time have caught a trout sporting another angler's fly. Research indicates that a trout has the ability to rid itself of a hook quite quickly, usually within a number of days with little or no negative effects.

Some trout, even of prodigious size, are landed quite easily whilst others will fight furiously in their attempts to escape. The magnitude of the fight is determined by many factors. A foul-hooked fish for example may be almost impossible to handle, but so too may one hooked conventionally. I once had a fish fight me for well over an hour, but this was partly due to the fact that I was using a tippet of less than 1.3kg and I was rather inexperienced. In the main, for New Zealand conditions I will rarely drop below a tippet of around 2kg (4X) rating. Indeed, in the case of some of the amazing materials now available line rated 4X (which is a measure of the line diameter), may have a breaking strain of up to 3kg, sufficient to hold most fish given reasonable topography. However, in the case of a wild, swift, backcountry stream liberally sprinkled with boulders and serious rapids I am much more inclined to use even 3.5kg tippets, taking a chance on spooking fish with the thicker nylon. Fluorocarbon, like tungsten beadheads has brought about something of a revolution in fly fishing and can definitely provide the angler with an edge over the person using conventional monofilament on very bright days and clear water due to its lower refractive index making it just a little more difficult for fish to detect.

In the long run though the skill of the angler and a modicum of good luck dictate how things will go once a fish is firmly attached. Once hooked the instinct of a wild trout is simply to attempt to distance itself from that which restrains it. The first run of even a relatively small fish may be quite breathtaking. It is simply foolhardy to attempt to check that run. A good quality reel with a well functioning drag will allow the fish to pull line off the spool smoothly and evenly. If necessary a little judicious thumbing of the spool may be called for. Many angling scribes claim that a fly reel serves little purpose other than that of storing line. I used to believe this myself but the experience of recent years has convinced me otherwise. A quality reel with a smoothly functioning drag system is nearly as important as a top quality rod. I have seen too many break-offs with inferior reels jamming inexplicably at crucial moments to take the myth seriously.

On the first run the rod tip should be held high so that the flexible tip absorbs the stresses. Many trout (browns included) will jump clear of the surface, often in spectacular fashion. If the fish is still attached after a number of heart-stopping events of this nature the chances are that it is really well hooked. To a degree the sage advice to "bow to the fish" when it jumps is correct for this is frequently the moment when the tippet is snapped or the extra pressure is just enough to pull the hook from the fish's mouth. Reducing the pressure at this moment is often crucial. It is important too to avoid as much as possible allowing the line to slacken as a lightly hooked fish will often come off at this point, especially with barbless hooks.

Years ago I was involved in a US television production entitled *Fly Fishing The World*. The programme filmed by the ESPN television group films celebrities fly fishing in many exotic fly fishing locations all around the world and is said to be hugely popular in the United States. I was asked to guide the team at the time of their visit to Nelson where they were hosted by Motueka River Lodge. I was a novice guide in those days but I endeavoured to do my best. Only two days were dedicated to filming and the host of the show was at great pains to inform me that we "had to get some excellent footage in the can", insinuating that I would be held personally responsible if we failed. The pressure this added was almost unbearable. Sleep did not come easily the night before our first outing.

The first episode was filmed on the Motueka River on a grey, drizzly day and didn't get off to the best of starts when the celebrity, in this case Richard Moll, a US comedy actor, hooked a fish on one of his practice casts before the cameras were rolling. The fish, a very good one too, came off after a minute or two, which was probably for the best really as it was far and away the biggest hooked that day. Despite being rather a novice Richard subsequently hooked and landed a few smaller fish and seemed happy with that, but the producer and host of the show, John Barrett was not content and decided to fish himself, as he often did if things were a bit slow. He finally caught and released a pretty nice brown and this sequence got on the show.

The next day dawned brilliantly fine so Syd Deaker duly arrived in his Hughes 500 to transport us all into the Karamea River for a sequence on wilderness fishing. It took two trips to get the whole crew on site. I had chosen a favourite run not far from Silvermine Creek and was not disappointed to discover a number of fish feeding well close to where we landed. By this time it was 10.00am and the situation was complicated by the fact that Richard, a delightful character incidentally, had to be back at the lodge by 2.00pm to catch a flight to Australia that evening. Under the circumstances John Barrett took it upon himself to try for the first fish just in case Richard was unsuccessful. At least they would have some footage to work with.

After what seemed an age Barrett was ready to fish and the cameras were rolling. The preparations seemed interminable and must have taken a full 40 minutes. I was acutely aware of the time ticking away. Fortunately Barrett could fish and he had little difficulty hooking one of the large trout I had spotted straight away. All seemed to be going well until suddenly the line went slack. Convinced that the fish had come off Barrett let out a barrage of language which would have made the proverbial trooper blush. Disgustedly he slapped the line on the water and really threw a tantrum. Not a word was spoken as, still swearing, he slowly and disconsolately wound the line in only to discover that there was still a fish attached. It was a case of "roll'em" again and after some time a magnificent fish of over 3kg was eventually landed, showing the importance of keeping a tight line as it is not unusual for a fish to swim towards the angler, especially in a big, slow flowing pool. This one could have so easily have been lost.

A trout being beached on a sandy shore. If the fish jumped about on this shore it would be less likely to be injured than if the bed was composed of large cobbles or rocks.

There was an interesting sequel to this event. While the two ESPN cameras stopped filming when it appeared that the fish had been lost, Syd, our pilot had continued to film from the background with his trusty camcorder. He has the entire sequence, complete with sound effects on video. Of course the "cussing" was expertly edited out of the show which appeared on TV. After a few lost fish Richard finally landed a really nice one just minutes before he had to step into the helicopter.

With experience, playing and landing even a very big trout is normally not too difficult, but occasionally one is stretched to the utmost by a fish determined to make good its escape. I have at times been "taken to the cleaners" by such a specimen, unable to ever really gain the upper hand. So be it. We should salute such fish and wish them well.

The majority of trout can be landed quite quickly by the application of sidestrain. While some anglers employ a technique involving rapid changes of rod position in order to confuse and keep the fish off balance there are dangers implicit as the constant movement from one side to the other is apt to loosen the hook's grip and may result in it coming free. I strongly advocate downstream sidestrain. By keeping the rod held to the side and maintaining a healthy bend whilst walking downstream it is often possible to have even a very feisty fish in the net in minutes.

Many fish are lost right at the net. For this reason many anglers prefer to do the netting themselves — not the easiest thing to do, especially with a long leader. At all times try first to net fish headfirst as a sudden burst of energy will often thrust the fish forward into the waiting net. Trout are front heavy so that when the net is lifted the fish is most likely to fall further into it. An absolute "no no" is stabbing at the fish with the net. Nothing will panic a trout more and a panicked fish will either break off or cause the fight to be prolonged, sometimes by many minutes. Ideally the fish should be netted by an accomplice with the trout being led to the stationary, waiting net. The netter should be positioned downstream taking advantage of anything which can afford cover, eg a large boulder. If it is necessary to net the fish in deeper water the angler should exercise patience to a point where the fish is immobile on or very close to the surface. The net should then be drawn up under the fish.

If the landing area is smooth with fine gravel or sand it is often preferable to beach the catch. If the fish is to be released it should not be dragged up onto rocks as it can do itself serious damage. As mentioned earlier it is possible to beach trout quite easily by keeping well back from the water's edge and keeping firm pressure on when the fish is heading shorewards. Be vigilant though and let the pressure off if it re-aligns itself facing away from the shore as it will strenuously avoid capture if possible.

A very large jack-fish being returned to a river. Fish of this quality should all be returned — they are the best breeding stock and part of a small age class that would take at least five years and absolutely ideal conditions to be replaced.

We have found that a trout inverted in the net on the ground is much easier to handle. The struggles often ease right off allowing the angler a brief moment of time to remove the hook. Again, try to avoid unnecessary handling. Squeezing the body or touching the gills is a cardinal sin as either action may result in injury and death later. Keeping it in the water will increase the chance of survival. Studies have found that larger fish are better equipped to survive the rigours of being played and landed than smaller ones. I recall an incident of which I am not proud which bears this out. I was fishing a small blackberry and scrub-lined stream near Nelson and over the space of just an hour or so I hooked, landed and released around a dozen fish. Most were in the 0.25–0.5kg category with a couple around a kilo. I thought I had released them all quite carefully. But I was somewhat chagrined to find three or four dead fish as I splashed my way back down the stream. It made me re-examine my landing and releasing technique carefully. I now prefer to use a net and remove the hook without even touching the fish if possible.

Much has been written about releasing trout but the basic principles are simple. The fish should be released as soon as possible. As most fish will go into a form of shock they should be cradled gently in the current until they choose to swim off of their own accord. Don't be in a hurry to move on. You owe it to the fish to do everything to ensure its survival. Even then watch carefully as it is possible for a seemingly fully recovered fish to turn belly-up. This is especially true in summer when water temperatures are high and there is less dissolved oxygen. In rivers where large eels are prevalent look out for them as I have seen eels actually attack recovering trout and even harass them whilst still being played. If a trout is being kept for food kill it quickly with at least one sharp tap to the head with a heavy object, preferably a rock.

Like golf, fly fishing is an immensely addictive, engrossing pastime. Similarly, whilst the bare basics are relatively easy to master, taking things to a higher plane requires serious commitment. My own, often frustrating journey from complete novice to something approaching competence is a case in point. I frequently encountered impediments in my earlier years. Indeed, with little guidance but plenty of opportunity by virtue of where I lived during that time I stumbled fitfully rather than attained skill by smooth progression. Taureans have a reputation for stubbornness. I'm no exception and if I want something badly enough I'll relentlessly plug away with an obstinate resolve to succeed. Fly fishing fascinated me totally. By a combination of trial and error, a little timely tuition and many hours spent on the water I slowly but surely made progress.

Some books proved incredibly helpful but I soon came to the

conclusion that nothing beats quality instruction. I believe implicitly in keeping things relatively simple. A good teacher should do likewise. By breaking things down into easy steps they make sense. All the theory in the world cannot replace the actual doing though. If I may be so bold as to make suggestions in the context of this chapter they are as follows. Firstly, learn and reinforce the basics first. Secondly, seek advice and if possible accompany experienced anglers at every possible opportunity. Watch, learn and copy. Finally, just get out there frequently and in all conditions, but never lose sight of the fact that it's meant to be fun.

Chapter 8 : A Host Of Techniques

New Zealanders have long been proud of their pioneer heritage. Many of us can trace our roots right back to the very early days of European settlement. Something in the nature of those adventurous souls who sought a new life in this then raw and untamed environment seems to have rubbed off on "Kiwis" of all ethnic backgrounds. Along with this fiercely independent, "give anything a go" attitude, which is still just as prevalent today, is an ability to adapt and "make do". Indeed New Zealanders have a reputation internationally for their ability to improvise and invent, and it is no surprise to find Kiwis at the top in many fields. We have a remarkably proud history in this regard, arguably second to none considering our miniscule population. Necessity has been the mother of invention, to coin the adage. To a degree this attitude has influenced the sport of fly fishing because of the very uniqueness of our situation.

Trout and salmon are not endemic to this country, but one could be forgiven for thinking that they were, considering the remarkable success of their acclimatisation here. Our waterways are subtly different from those in other parts of the world and our trout are different too. In Europe and the United States natural trout populations tend to comprise mainly of large populations of (by our standards) small trout. Many US anglers of my acquaintance are astonished to discover that in many of our backcountry streams trout actually seem to get bigger as one progresses upstream, in direct contrast to the situation in their country. There, altitude means a long, often icy winter, and limited feeding opportunities. While it cannot be taken as a general rule it is not at all unusual to encounter some of our larger fish in the very last pools of some rivers before they rise so steeply and become too rough to be viable trout habitats at all. We are blessed too with streams of exceptional purity and clarity, and extremely clear air by northern hemisphere standards. The sheer harshness of the environment appears to ensure that only a few fish — the fittest and strongest and best able to adapt will survive. As we experience relatively mild winters these large trout are able to feed all year round and maintain reasonable body weights despite the rigours of reproduction and smaller food intake during the colder months.

These factors have led to the development of specific tactics for catching trout in this country. To a degree the stalking technique is uniquely a New Zealand method and I can still recall the bemusement of some of my earliest clients when I explained that we would walk the stream, searching the water carefully with the aid of polarised glasses to find a fish before we would make a cast. One or two looked at me with total amazement, but it didn't take too long, normally, to convince them that this was the way to fish here. Of course the majority of visiting anglers had heard all about stalking and came here just to enjoy this somewhat new and novel challenge.

We have developed techniques in keeping with our tradition of innovation. One of course is the upstream, stalking method which we have outlined at length. Because of the clarity of the water we have learned to fish with long leaders, fine in still conditions or with a gentle upstream breeze, but so important if our super wary fish are going to be fooled. As aforementioned I have long subscribed to the "keep it simple" school. Some aspects though, deserve meticulous preparation. We now enjoy the luxury of combining our specific techniques and the rigs we have designed with the very best of rod, reel, line, leader and tippet combinations from manufacturers all over the world. As an example, I own graphite rods made and/or designed in New Zealand, the United Kingdom and the United States. Some materials have become virtually obsolete. Just to remind me of this I recently took the two remaining hollow fibreglass rods I own out of the cupboard and had a few casts with each, loaded with the appropriate weight line. I have to admit to being shocked — initially by the sheer weight difference, but also by the unresponsiveness of the glass compared with carbon fibre. No wonder it is relatively easy to start novice anglers off on the right path these days. I make no apologies when I contend that the very best fly rods in the world originate from the United States. But the rest are learning very quickly with the top New Zealand-made rods being of fine quality.

A great deal has been written about specific rigs in recent years, and most of it is helpful. Innovations which I've found particularly useful are the leader to fly line loop systems which enable swift changes to be made when necessary. While I still like monofilament nylon tapered leaders, I'm beginning to appreciate the usefulness of the Airflo poly leader system, especially in situations where head winds are common, as they do seem to turn over better than mono in windy conditions. While many anglers, especially North Island rainbow trout fishers still prefer to fish with a single piece of monofilament in order to get their heavily weighted rigs down to the bottom quickly in deep, fast water, tapered leaders are much easier to roll out and to provide a natural presentation where one is necessary. In smaller stream brown trout fisheries tapered leaders are virtually indispensable.

Some dedicated fishers spend the long winter nights constructing flies and making up tapered leaders. Fly tying is fun, and if you have a talent for it a great way of saving money. I like to make some of my own nymphs but have never really come close to mastering the art of tying dries. As I seem to have little ability I prefer to leave it to experts like my old friend Pete Carty if I am able to twist his arm! As for meticulously preparing hand-tied leaders — sorry but its not my idea of fun. Each to their own. There is no doubt though that correctly tied, knotted leaders are great to fish with. The hand-tied variety can be obtained from many US tackle dealers. I prefer to start with a short, say nine foot tapered leader of perhaps 2X tippet and

The trout pictured has been hooked on a single nymph rig. The white yarn indicator is clearly visible about 0.8 metres up the line.

add pieces of tippet material with a blood knot to achieve the length and breaking strain I desire for a particular situation. On some occasions I will start with a 12 foot tapered leader, especially in situations requiring delicacy, but also on days with a gentle upstream breeze. It's not a bad idea to have a few of these of different lengths in the vest ready for use if necessary, but I will frequently fish for days with the original leader, making sure I start each outing with fresh tippets. Some days see me chopping and changing constantly for varying circumstances. A stiff headwind requires a change to a much shorter, stiffer leader as long leaders soon prove quite unmanageable. The key is to check, check, check, especially in windy conditions as loops form quite easily. A fish lost due to a wind knot or frayed nylon is inexcusable.

As the majority of our fishing is done casting upstream with a single or double nymph rig it is appropriate that we examine these first. The simplest system, and still a highly effective one is to fish with just one weighted nymph with an indicator placed at a suitable distance up the leader.

I will often match the length of my tippet to correspond with the distance from the nymph I consider the optimum. While some subscribe to placing the indicator as close as 30cm or even less from the nymph in shallow water I do not really accept this. In the main a metre or just a little less would be the minimum for me. If I'm really concerned that the indicator is going to spook the fish and I can see clearly what the fish is doing I'll dispense with the indicator altogether. In very bright, clear conditions and in situations where fish have been subjected to considerable pressure it may be necessary to do this but timing the strike can be tricky. Placing the indicator just above the tippet knot makes good sense as it can't slip down any further.

My favourite nymphing rig comprises two nymphs and an indicator. Just what combination of nymphs is most effective is debatable. The system employed on big rivers like the Tongariro which incorporate a large, heavy, attractor like a Glo-bug with a much smaller, more natural looking pattern such as some form of mayfly nymph seems to work well. To a degree it is the system I employ in the South Island, but replacing the large Glo-bug (or similar) with a quite modest sized Tungsten Beadhead,with a similar or smaller sized lightly weighted or unweighted mayfly or caddis imitation as a trailer.

Towards the end of the 2005 summer I took a short drive from my home to the Arnold River which runs out of Lake Brunner. It was a beautiful day but the river was very swollen after heavy rain and the colour of dark tea. I wasn't too worried as I just felt like a bit of a break after working seven days a week for a while. Choosing a stretch in the lower reaches which wasn't horribly choked by willows (a serious problem on this fine river) I strode right up to the head of a major run which had an excellent looking eye. I had to negotiate a substantial side stream with the slipperiest bottom of cobblestone-sized rocks imaginable. With some difficulty, as the water was very swift, I achieved the safety of a small, grassed island and started fishing with the aforementioned Tungsten Bead and a #14 Nelson Brown tied on a short trace off the bend of the hook. As the water was quite deep I had a white yarn indicator positioned about a metre and a half up the leader. Starting with short casts I commenced fishing my way up through the relatively quiet water, concentrating on the very obvious seam. I quickly sensed that there was little to be gained from fishing out beyond the seam as the full force of the current raged down, creating a very inhospitable habitat. Success was almost immediate. The indicator was literally snatched under the surface and a solid little brown of about 30cm jumped and cavorted about. I quickly drew it into the net and noted with interest that it had taken the Nelson Brown. I continued up the run taking seven or eight fish with two in the 1.5kg category, one of which accompanied me home. Every fish was taken on the little, lightly weighted Nelson Brown.

After a while the action began to ease off and I wondered if virtually all the fish present had seen enough of my combination. I decided to experiment. Off came the Tungsten Beadhead and on went a San Juan worm tied with a bright gold bead for some extra weight. As the floodwaters had been right up over the fields the previous day earthworms would in all likelihood be forming part of the diet of the resident fish. I re-attached the Nelson Brown, went back to the bottom of the run and started again. The results, while not quite as spectacular, were still very pleasing and I succeeded in landing a few more fish. There was literally nowhere else handy to try so I headed off home very content with the results of my brief foray. Interestingly each fish I landed had the little mayfly imitation in its jaw, causing me to wonder if the top nymph was simply acting as an attractor for the more natural attachment or as an additional source of weight to get the smaller nymph to the optimum depth. While I have not kept records to prove it I have found that the trailing nymph is taken far more frequently than the larger or more heavily weighted one, possibly in the ratio of 4:1 or greater. Of course it is possible that even a larger nymph on the trailer would attract more strikes simply because of its position and the more natural motion achieved.

We have experimented considerably with both combinations of nymphs and indicators. While some experienced anglers will claim that a "trailer" nymph must be tied off the eye, others will attest to the success of simply tying the trace off the bend of the hook. I have no particular preference and have enjoyed success with both methods. The latter though, does have the disadvantage of just occasionally slipping off barbless hooks. Some anglers prefer to fish one nymph tied off a completely different trace much as a dry fly would be. One method of tying a trace is to lengthen out one piece of tippet material to the desired length and tie it in with a blood knot.

Many anglers, Les included, prefer to use a dry fly as an indicator. This method can prove most effective as a dry fly seems less likely to scare wary fish than a yarn indicator and of course has the added advantage of giving fish an opportunity to choose the dry fly option, a bonus for the angler.

I fish with yarn indicators a great deal of the time. Poly yarn, impregnated with a suitable floatant works fine, but so does natural wool. I'll quite often stock up on this material from the wire fences of fields holding sheep. There are times when brightly coloured indicators are essential,

Six different rigs for fishing with nymphs.

A.   A dry fly and nymph combination with the dryfly on a dropper.

B.   A single nymph with indicator.,

C.   Two nymphs — the bottom one is connected to the upper with the tippet tied to the eye.

D.   Two nymphs — the trailer nymph is tied off the bend in the forward hook.

E.   A dry fly and nymph with the nymph tied off the eye of the surface fly.

F.   A dry fly and nymph. The nymph is tied off the bend in the hook of the dry fly.

though in the main I prefer plain white as long as I can see it clearly. There is a place for black indicators and I have used them extensively, especially late in the afternoon when surface glare becomes a problem. If fish appear to be spooked by the indicator then one should either fine it down, change colour or dispense with it altogether. I fish with the smallest practical indicator I can get away with, sometimes a mere wisp of material. But if you can only see it half the time it is on the water you are wasting your time. It must be visible throughout the drift or you will simply lose control and confidence in what you are doing and miss a vital take. Some anglers are very keen on indicator putty. As a rule I don't like it as it tends to sit right in the surface film, and like lead putty has an annoying tendency to come adrift during casting.

The trout in the net has taken a nymph. A dry fly indicator can be seen clearly about 1.3 metres up the line, hanging on a dropper.

When I first fished the Tongariro many years ago I scoffed at the size of the indicators being used there, but soon realised that they were essential considering the heavy terminal equipment being employed and the often turbulent, deep runs being fished. I confess to much frustration fishing the "Big T" at times as I was accustomed to using much more subtle equipment. I have observed the same situation in reverse when big water rainbow exponents come to the South Island armed with heavy rods, brightly coloured lines, exceptionally heavy nymphs and "feather duster" indicators. Some adjust quickly but others find the transition difficult.

The most important element of deep nymph fishing is getting the nymph down in the water column as quickly as possible. There are times when extra weight is required to achieve this. Sliding an extra bead down onto the top nymph can be remarkably effective as it adds weight and extra attractor power. Other methods include the aforementioned use of lead or lead substitute putty added to the leader. This substance is very useful and easy to apply. Lead shot on the leader is a time honoured method but it can be tricky to affix and very awkward to cast. However, split shot has saved the day for me with fish feeding on the bottom of very deep pools so many times that my use of it is very much a love-hate affair. Strip lead is also favoured by some. These latter methods are only useful where delicate presentation is not an issue. More and more I find that plumbing the depths produces results. Whereas once I would simply place deep pools in the "too hard basket" I rarely do so now.

On a backcountry river I once guided an Italian angler who taught me a thing or two about fishing for trout in very deep water. Silvio was a very accomplished angler and a lot of fun to be with. We spotted the monsters off a high bank in the very first pool we approached. There they lay, five in all like logs on the fine gravel bottom five or six metres down. We gazed in awe and Silvio became very animated as he had never seen trout quite like these before. I estimated the largest fish in the prime position near the top of the pool to be in the 5kg category and the rest all in excess of 3.5kg. Naturally my client wanted to have a shot at them. I tried to gently explain that because of the nature of the water they were in our chances were virtually nil, but he looked so crestfallen that I reluctantly agreed to him having a few casts.

"Show me your nymphs," he demanded and he selected a huge pattern which had actually been tied with a lump of split shot forming part of the body. Silvio proceeded to lob the "bomb" up the pool. I could literally see the thing descending through the silt free water. The fish took no notice of us even though I was absolutely sure they could see us from our exposed position on a rocky ledge above the pool. It was soon clear that the leader was not long enough so I had Silvio pull it in so I could make adjustments. I added at least another metre and away he went again. Time after time he lobbed rather than cast the rig up towards the head of the pool. After perhaps a dozen casts I fancied that one of the smaller fish had actually followed the nymph a short distance down the pool.

"Try it again Silvio," I suggested. "A bit further up if you can."

With a huge effort he tried again and this time I felt sure that another fish had a look but soon went back into its appointed place in the pecking order, and like all the others occasionally moved to the side taking invertebrates close to the bottom. I had just about given up hope and was gazing at the magnificent bluffs towering up on the other side of the valley when a scream of sheer joy rent the air. He had one. The wonderful sight of a big bend in the rod left me in no doubt about that. Now it was my turn to get excited as I knew that the fish was a big one, and I also recalled that in my tinkering with the leader I had deliberately gone for a very light tippet, from memory as light as 5X, to assist the nymph to get down in a hurry.

I'd heard that Italians were very excitable people but to his credit Silvio did a wonderful job and kept his head. Fortunately the fish chose to stay in the relatively obstruction-free pool and like nearly all really big trout I've encountered spent most of the time in the deepest part. One run downstream and it would have all been over as it was impossible to follow. After many heart-stopping minutes Silvio had coaxed the fish into a deep back-water near the tail of the pool. With some difficulty I was able to clamber down the rocky outcrop to a tiny ledge whilst Silvio stayed on the terrace well above my head. The gradually tiring trout just went round and round with the eddying current. Slowly but surely it came closer to the surface and to the shore with each circuit. Urging Silvio to exercise the utmost caution I awaited my chance. Finally it came and I was able to reach out just far enough for it to slide headfirst into the net. What a beauty! According to the net scale it weighed in at just under the magic 4.5kg or 10lb mark, but was still a fine prize — a short, deep, pale coloured jack — a relatively young fish I fancied as it was unscarred, with a small head and didn't sport the very pronounced kype of an older fish. A quick photo or two was taken and the tired fish returned to its haven. This was Silvio's largest brown trout. He'd actually taken a similar-sized rainbow on a previous trip to New Zealand but the capture of the brown in such circumstances was very special to him. He caught more fish over the next three days but nothing approached the size of his first deep water one.

Unfortunately, the New Zealand featured in the travel brochures publicising trout fishing almost always shows anglers wearing wide grins as they hold aloft large brown or rainbow trout. The water is always wonderfully clear and the sky blue. The truth of the matter is that it does rain, and its just as likely to fall in February as it is in the winter months of June or July. Rain can, and does occur in every month of the year, especially in the mountains which just happens to be where the best fishing is often to be had. While some waters are open year round the main season opens on October 1. October in this country, as every trout fisher will attest, is often very forgettable due to the frequent passage of frontal weather systems and distinctly wintry weather. However, every serious Kiwi angler looks forward to October 1 like Christmas, eagerly anticipating battles with fat trout. Alas, the reality is often different.

Often anglers have to cope with difficult conditions like the strong wind pictured — on a stream or lake.

I can recall struggling with conditions of wind and freezing rain on so many occasions that now I almost expect the opening day to be inclement. However, just to prove that we are real anglers we usually sally forth despite the conditions.

There are trout to be caught. We know that, but connecting with them in murky, high waters can pose enormous problems. This is the time for the positive attitude we often allude to. Unless rivers are totally flooded there are still great opportunities, albeit somewhat limited. It's time for lateral thinking. I would rather take my chances in very murky water than with a severe downstream wind. If the chances of spotting fish seem very low then fishing blind it will be. Reading the water becomes a vital skill. One needs to ask oneself where a trout would shelter in near flood conditions. Sometimes high water limits the options in the angler's favour. Rainbows especially don't like really discoloured water and will frequently be found in numbers close to where a clearer tributary stream runs in, a prime place for browns too. Throughout I have recounted anecdotes about Al, my somewhat difficult, often tetchy Californian. On one of his trips to New Zealand he brought his adult son Bob. Why he did so escapes me as father and son spent much of their time together on the river arguing. It seems that the conflict continued back at the lodge so I wasn't surprised when Bob cut short his trip and returned to the States after just a few days.

The fishing on this trip was pretty good on the whole. With money not being a problem the pair spent up big on helicopter time and caught some excellent fish. But, part way into the seven day trip the heavens opened and I was forced to admit defeat as the Motueka was just mud. "Not a problem," said Al when I went round to deliver the bad news, as being a big wine buff he was looking for a chance to do a little tasting of the local vintages. The lodge owner duly took him and Bob off around the wineries but not before I had them agree to be back at the lodge at 2.00pm as I suspected that we might be able to find some clear water somewhere.

The appointed time arrived and father and son, whilst hesitant and feeling somewhat mellow after their wine tasting decided that they would just give it a couple of hours. This pleased me as it meant that I would get paid for the day. In their absence I'd done a bit of a reconnaisance and found a substantial sidestream not far away that looked promising. It too was very high but much, much clearer than the main river which was the colour of dark chocolate and likely to stay that way for days. Anyway, in we went, threading our way around shrubby, inundated willows. The small stream very quickly merged with the larger one and was soon swallowed up in the murk of the main river. I noted with interest though that a clearish eye had formed at the confluence and a narrow strip of relatively clear water continued downstream for at least 50 metres. It was definitely fishable.

I soon had them equipped with double nymph rigs on short leaders of around three metres. In such water conditions neither delicacy or finesse was required so I was not concerned by the sloppier than normal casting technique, no doubt a product of their middle of the day wine consumption. While they were working the lower end of the fishable water I decided to wander up towards the top of the run, hoping that I might be able to spot a fish, as even one each would be considered a good day in the circumstances. At a point about 20 metres below the confluence I stopped abruptly, transfixed, as there, just a few metres from the shore I saw a large set of jaws break the surface and suck in some surface morsel. As I watched, very much "on point" now my heart leapt as there was another rise, and another and another. The narrow strip of water seemed to be full of fish either rising or taking sub-surface with a pronounced swirl. Trying to stay calm I marched quickly back to where the "boys" were flailing away with their nymph rigs and suggested, nay, commanded that they follow me upstream. Even Al, not renowned for his eyesight was impressed.

"Wow, just look at those lunkers Bob."

I soon had Al rigged up with a large, bushy dry fly. The way the fish were feeding I didn't think more subtle methods were required, and so it proved. Al's first cast was in the "ball park" and quickly snapped up by a large, eager brown which took off downstream at a great rate. Al was now no stranger to sidestraining and did a very good job of bringing a fine fish to the bank within a few minutes. The jack of about 2.5kg had no apparent desire to head off into the murky floodwaters, which was just as well as our rocky shoreline very quickly merged into at least a kilometre stretch of impenetrable flooded willows.

Like father like son. Bob wasted no time in evening the score with a similar fish. An hour later at three very nice fish apiece we had pretty much exhausted the possibilities. There were more fish in evidence but the bad vibes had spread and the remaining fish were not to be fooled.

"No good eh," grinned the lodge proprietor when we returned just before 5pm.

My clients simply ignored him and headed for one of the bottles of expensive sauvignon blanc they had purchased earlier that day. A celebration was definitely in order.

While few days have such a fairytale ending as this, flooded rivers should not be rejected as unfishable. It is logical that trout will head for cover during a flood event. When surveying a seriously swollen river one has to isolate the possible holding water. We have enjoyed success in some very marginal circumstances at times, simply because we were not intimidated by them. If there is one positive to be taken from such conditions it is that it is simple to nominate the water which definitely won't produce. Trout seek relative comfort during a flood. While it may mean spending the time on the bottom of a deep pool well away from the surface turbulence for some, for others it may mean simply slipping away into dense vegetation. While anglers often curse willows crowding waterways there is no doubt at all that these are places of refuge. Other fish seek cover in very shallow edge water or under overhanging banks, pockets or right up in normally miniscule sidestreams. These temporary safe houses can be exploited by the positive thinking angler.

One also has to be prepared to adapt technique in high, discoloured water. In very murky conditions trout are very unlikely to see a weighted nymph. Conversely, some fish will dine on surface items as these will be silhouetted quite clearly. We have enjoyed some wonderful dry fly fishing as a result. Another method, and one which our American friends have great confidence in, is to work a big, dark coloured streamer fly such as a Woolly Bugger very slowly through potential fish holding water. Large, predatory browns are sometimes very impressed by such offerings, much as they are by streamers fished through clear water on the blackest of nights.

There are of course times when fishing is right out of the question, but in my experience, apart from during really serious flood events this is most likely to be during severe gales. I have also learned to keep away from water, during a thunderstorm, especially whilst carrying a carbon fibre rod, one of the best conductors of electricity known.

The fickleness of New Zealand weather is legendary. I was frequently asked by my guided clients to specify a time of the year when it didn't rain. Of course it was impossible to give such an assurance. One of my clients always timed his trips here for February, in the belief that blue skies were almost guaranteed. Unfortunately he often got it wrong. Some Americans find it difficult to accept that summers here are very unpredictable as they are used to cloudless skies and near identical conditions for weeks on end in their country. The weather in our island paradise is extremely variable. Indeed, some of the worst flooding I have seen has occurred in mid-summer.

This then implies a need for adaptability in terms of method, and this is partly why I have outlined a range of techniques here. An open mind and a willingness to think "outside the square" is imperative, for just when we think we have seen it all something will occur to derail the best of theories.

Chapter 9 : Fishing Blind —
A Misnomer

We have made reference to the importance of attitude in fly fishing. If ever there was a situation where positive thinking is critical it is whilst fishing "blind." As we shall see the term is really not particularly apt in many respects. Actually, the term "prospecting" may be more suitable but still does not really capture the essence of one of the more fascinating aspects of fly fishing. For the purpose of this book we will stick with the term "blind fishing" as it is the one which most people understand. Just as the experienced spin fisher knows full well that his chosen method is not just "chuck and chance" as many disparaging fly fishers would describe it, but a truly legitimate form of the sport of fishing for trout, so too is the method known as blind fishing using dry fly, nymph or wet fly.

True, some anglers do fish "blind" with little confidence in what they are doing and lacking the knowledge to read the water effectively enough to enjoy more than rare success. While spin fishers are arguably more inclined to err in this respect I've observed many fly fishers exhibit similarly haphazard technique. Occasionally, sheer doggedness and perseverance results in a hook-up but the results are usually disappointing. There was a time when I was guilty of fishing thus when conditions precluded sight fishing, and in retrospect frequently fished very large areas of unproductive water without much commitment and lack of success. Flogging away for hours with low expectations is somewhat depressing, and quite futile.

There are a few issues which need to be understood about blind fishing. While I will expand upon the pros and cons of sight fishing versus blind fishing in Chapter 11 suffice it to state that in the ideal world we would probably all prefer to fish to a specific target and eliminate a great deal of what really amounts to casting practice. But conditions are often far from perfect in the world of trout fishing. Consequently, if even a modicum of success is to be enjoyed we have to fish blind. It may come as a surprise to some that there are situations where I actually prefer to fish blind even when conditions appear to be ideal for sight fishing.

If fishing a river with a better than average head of fish, especially one with long stretches of joggly water and moderate depth it can actually be counterproductive to attempt sight fishing as many fish will be missed altogether which it may have been possible to cover with a series of long drifts over the target area. To simply walk past because no fish are visible is very poor technique.

Stalking Trout, our first book together, and part one of this volume may have given the impression that Les and I are almost exclusively committed to sight fishing. While it is certainly our preferred method we both often gain great pleasure from fishing either dry fly or nymph, or a combination of both in water which we suspect strongly harbours some feeding, and therefore catchable fish.

An angler probing high probability water (water that has a high chance of holding trout). In this instance the angler is fishing at the top of a run, in the eye of the pool. The angler and photographer landed five fish from the small area shown.

Two anglers resting beside low probability water – very swift with no pockets or cover for trout.

As a guide I would estimate that at least 70% of the time I had my clients fishing high probability water by blind fishing techniques, sometimes with amazing results. My beloved Motueka River, which I often refer to because it is the one on which I have fished more than any other, is a case in point. Arguably one of the most fickle and frustrating brown trout rivers on the planet it has the ability to become hugely productive, sometimes without warning. The analogy of a tap or light switch being turned on or off is most apt when referring to this river. I have seen a totally "dead" river come to life during the course of a day or for this to happen inexplicably after a succession of really hard days. The converse is also true. Influencing factors include rising or falling barometric pressure, a rising or falling river level, prolific hatches of a specific stream insect or the appearance of a certain terrestrial. Many people who have fished in the now famous One Fly Competition held in Nelson each March will have experienced the good fortune of striking the peak of the passion vine hopper hatch. This small, fat bodied, terrestrial with delta shaped wings vainly attempts to destroy the leaves of the ubiquitous old man's beard (*clematis vitalba*), a major plant pest in this area. The passion hopper looks like a tiny ball of white fluff in its early stages and then takes the shape described above. At the peak of the hopper's abundance the normally wary Motueka browns can become ridiculously easy to fool with a good imitation of this curious insect. At times the fish may be observed rising in feedlines where the bulk of the hoppers are concentrated but I have also enjoyed success by fishing the imitation dry even when there was little evidence of rising fish.

I once saw one angler take 23 browns on the Motueka, each weighing over 1.5kg by the simple method of fishing riffly water at the head of each long run we encountered during the course of the day. Some of those fish were taken from water less than 30 centimetres deep. He used nothing but a single, moderately weighted #16 Pheasant Tail nymph. Curiously, as a heavy hatch of mayflies occurred for most of the day, hardly a fish rose to the floating duns or emergers even though the former sailed down in their thousands. The fish stayed on the bottom, feasting on what was obviously a veritable banquet of nymphs as they were washed downstream. I have enjoyed this sort of action on many occasions and only a small fraction of those fish would have been obvious to an angler deliberately sight fishing as surface glare, a disturbed water surface and uniformly brown, algae-coated rocks made for difficult sight fishing.

Blind fishing is not necessarily a technique for just dull, rainy or windy days when sight fishing is difficult or near impossible. Especially early and late in the season the angle of light is ideal for sight fishing for only a few hours of the day. This is certainly the case during April, or where the regulations permit, during the month of May. Sight fishing can be very hard unless all the factors are favourable. It then becomes a case of percentage fishing. I recall visiting the upper Karamea River on a sort of "busman's holiday" with some friends one Easter break, which that year was very late — well into April. To cut down on weight in the helicopter as there were four of us with a lot of gear, including rifles I foolishly left my full length stocking foot waders behind, a decision I was to rue as each day dawned clear and cold and wading through bouldery runs, sometimes to well above waist level, was extremely unpleasant as I feel the cold badly. This section of river was in almost perpetual shadow at this time of year for much of the day, and worse from an angling viewpoint, it was half in shadow and half in sunlight when the sun did finally penetrate into the narrow, bush-clad valley for an hour or so in the middle of the day.

One of my companions was a fly fisher, but exclusively that — a dry fly man who had little experience with nymphs. We fished together the first morning before the cold forced us back to the hut for a hot soup. Between us we managed to catch and release a rather thin and somewhat forlorn looking jack of close to 3kg which actually took a small Elk Hair Caddis dry, but all the other fish we saw were not to be fooled and not surprisingly as they were cruising round restlessly in the deep, still pools which are common here. This late in the season they had seen a lot of other fishermen and totally ignored our offerings. Over lunch a couple of DOC workers I happened to know turned up and were to share the hut with us for the remaining three days of our stay.

"Aha", exclaimed Russell, "we'll dine on trout tonight eh Graeme."

"Of course," I replied, but not with the confidence I might have exuded in different circumstances. However, the challenge had been issued and a certain amount of pride was at stake. Ray, my companion of the morning was content to spend the afternoon reading and squashing sandflies and the other two elected to look for a deer up a nearby side creek, so after a hearty lunch I headed off downstream on the track for an hour or so. Wandering along through the cool mixed beech and podocarp forest I pondered the situation. As I saw it a lot of the fish were residing in the big pools, and I suspect more interested in pairing up for spawning than feeding too avidly. Big browns are always difficult in this situation but I recalled other seasons when I had come across good numbers of fish in the faster water too. These latter were completely different from their largely resident pool dwelling brethren. They were often smaller, bright, silvery hen fish in top condition which I suspect were moving upriver from their normal residences in the slower flowing earthquake lakes of the middle and lower river to spawn. The main Karamea and its tributaries were often full of these fish late in the season. Hopefully I might encounter some of them in the faster runs and riffles.

By the time I reached a long, bouldery run some distance above the swing-bridge upstream from the gorge there was little sun on the water but initially I elected to sight fish. I spied one nice fish sitting upstream of a large, exposed boulder and popped a dry fly up above it. The fly didn't even get a second glance as the fish took off as if stung by one of the far too numerous wasps in evidence. Phew, this was going to be a challenge. When it happened twice more I knew that I had to change my tactics. Off went the dry and on went a #14 weighted Hare and Copper and a tiny wisp of white indicator. Now I targeted the fast runs in mid-stream. Perching precariously up on top of the large granite boulders I prospected the water I couldn't see into well. From past experience this section of river was also populated with some of the biggest eels it is possible to imagine so I kept glancing nervously around my bare legs as I waded from rock to rock and recalled the time I casually mentioned to a bare-legged American client who was playing a fish that the large eel swimming around his legs was probably harmless. Despite the opinion of doubters it is possible to walk on water!

I had a good feeling about the stretch I was fishing despite not being able to see into the water. Success was almost immediate. Within minutes the indicator just stopped and when I lifted instinctively I felt the weight of a nice fish, a bar of solid silver which proceeded to perform spectacular somersaults down the pool leading me a merry dance back to where I'd entered the water. The jumps soon took their toll and I was able to drag it around behind a boulder and into a shallow bay and up onto a small sandy beach. This one was destined for the pot. A quick post mortem showed that the fat hen of about 1.8kg was gorged with free swimming caddis pupa and a number of mayfly nymphs. The Hare and Copper had been an apt choice. The fish was carefully wrapped in a plastic bag and popped into my day bag. I wanted one more to ensure that fish was definitely on the menu that evening.

It wasn't long in coming — a near clone of the first from just a few metres further upstream. There was no lack of fish, and I must have caught and released another four or five of similar size in the next couple of hours before plodding happily back up the track to the hut and a convivial evening. Not one of these fish did I see first. Blind fishing had proved its worth yet again. A sad postscript to this story is that one of the DOC workers, Russell Griebel, lost his life along with Bob Waldie when the hut they were in was washed into the upper Motueka River during a flash flood a year or two later.

To fish blind with confidence it is essential to examine the water carefully first. Some water holds fish most of the time, some does part of the time and a whole lot very rarely, or if it does is difficult to fish. It is necessary to attempt to eliminate as much of the latter type from our attention as possible to narrow the odds. As a general rule it is sensible to concentrate the effort on approximately the top 25% more or less of a given run.

A section of river with a high probability of holding a trout – in the froth line on a low gradient, grassland stream. Where froth (bubbles) accumulates so does surface food. Trout target areas like this often.

Another high probability section of water. In this case the angler has hooked a trout that fed ahead of a boulder, however, many other large obstructions litter the bed with deep water nearby. A trout (or two) could lie in one of many places in this section of river. Great blind fishing water.

While there are undoubtedly some fish in residence in other portions the upper section is often more productive as this is where invertebrate drift is being washed into the run and the surface disturbance created by the faster moving water makes it much easier to avoid lining fish. But it is important not to simply rush up to the top of the run without examining the scene carefully. The presence of a submerged log, boulders, bank extension or tributary can radically alter the whole situation.

If ever there was a time for reading the water carefully this is it. Many anglers, especially relative novices and those accustomed to only small streams are often intimidated by big waters. But big waters can still be broken down into specific types of water after close examination. While I might go straight to the areas I know to be the most productive on rivers I've fished before I'm much more circumspect now on first acquaintance. It is very definitely a case of treading very carefully as productive little sub zones within a relatively uninspiring appearing section of stream can produce surprises. In the main I tend to eliminate tail out areas. While occasional bonuses occur I have found these areas somewhat devoid of larger fish and difficult to attack without the almost inevitable drag.

A pool with high, medium and low probability water. There would be a high chance of trout holding in the top section, a medium chance of fish being in the middle section but the expectation of a large fish feeding in the downstream portion would be low.

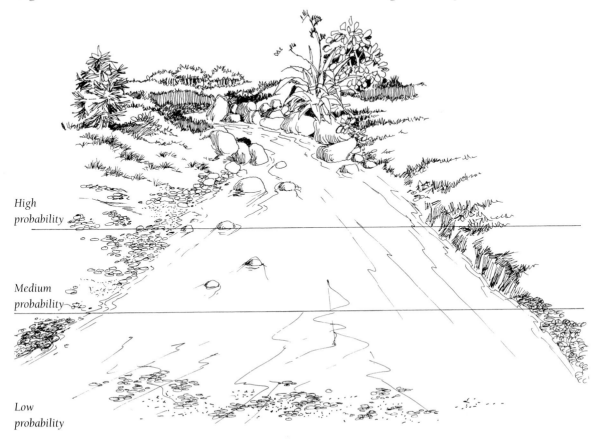

High
probability

Medium
probability

Low
probability

Moving up, towards the middle of the run, I'm much more optimistic as some of the most productive fishing is to be found here, especially over a bottom comprised of large substrate in the form of cobbles, big rocks or even solid rock outcrops. Large, relatively undefined and somewhat featureless runs with a bottom of small or very fine substrate like sand or very fine gravel, especially in shallow water, usually have little interest for me but as soon as the depth increases and strata increases in size forming pockets and hollows I'm on alert.

If I'm serious about blind fishing any given run I will frequently begin prospecting from about halfway up, especially if it is difficult to see the bottom due to surface disturbance, a sign of uneven strata and potential fish holding pockets. Time of year dictates choice of rig. On larger waters I will normally fish a nymph and dry fly rig or a double nymph rig (see illustrations). However, in mid-summer or at any time when I suspect that fish are likely to be interested in surface flies (whether of stream or terrestrial origin) I will confidently start with a dry, with one simple proviso and that is simply that the fly is highly visible. If there is a significant hatch of caddis my choice of fly is normally a caddis pattern such as the highly effective Elk Hair Caddis, ensuring that it is as close as possible in size to the naturals. If mayflies are in abundance I'll opt for a Parachute Adams or similar, if necessary tied with a fluoro coloured hackle for the best possible visibility. If the fly cannot be seen at all times on the water then you are wasting your time and you should change. Just occasionally, in low, glary light situations that may occur in the late afternoon a black hackle is actually the most visible.

During the exciting cicada time which varies from year to year and from region to region large flies come into their own. In my experience the close imitations of cicadas sold in tackle stores across the country are often dull hued and hard to see on the water. I've had much more success with large Stimulators or patterns like Turks Tarantula or Carty's GT. When the cicadas, hoppers and other large terrestrials abound almost any large, bulky pattern will suffice.

I have also enjoyed great success, especially fishing for rainbows, but browns too with a Royal Wulff. I will never forget one memorable day in north-west Nelson when two of us landed twelve magnificent browns. All were taken with this wonderful dry fly and most were not spotted first. Brian and I had been hut-bound for some days and the river had been up and down a number of times as a succession of thunderstorms rolled around the mountains. Finally the torrential downpours ceased and the skies went silent. Dawn broke to reveal a layer of fog low down on the bush, normally a positive sign, and so it proved as the first hints of blue began to show as we left the hut around 9.00am. The river, though still running high had receded unbelievably quickly overnight and while still carrying a moderate sediment load was more the colour of tea than anything. We couldn't access the first run above the hut easily as the water was in the scrub and flowing swiftly but by heading up the track parallelling the river for a few hundred metres we were able to make our way, albeit with some difficulty to the very top of the run. I've rarely felt more confident of success than I did right then. The main river, quite narrow at this point, thundered past but a substantial area of quiet water, studded with large, lichen-encrusted granite boulders and the odd wispy coprosma bush had formed creating what looked like a haven for trout as really it was the only relatively quiet part of the entire run. The stretch was around twenty metres long and up to ten metres wide at its widest point. A reasonable current flowed through sucking invitingly around the large boulders.

I had no hesitation in tying on a Royal Wulff and suggested to Brian that he do likewise. My first cast was made right against the bank and I thought that it would go unnoticed until a large snout and set of jaws broke through the surface just a few metres upstream. In my surprise I struck far too quickly and pulled the fly right out of the fish's mouth. "Damn." Cursing, I invited Brian to take over. Just two or three casts later and a little further up and out a near identical head lifted almost clean out of the water and sucked in the fly. Brian was much more composed and waited for a respectable length of time before striking. There was no mistake this time and he was soon playing a typical jack of around 2.5kg which was not inclined to head out into the turbulent main stream. It was soon landed and released after being duly admired and photographed.

The action was just beginning. We took another three out of the remainder of the eye before proceeding to probe a long run of largely pocket water with similar results. Occasionally we had to detour on the track a little way before finding a route down to the water's edge once more. Only in the early afternoon when the water had cleared and dropped significantly did we start to actually spot fish. When we came to a point where our progress upriver was barred by a substantial bluff, we decided to retrace our steps back to the hut to toast our success. I've fished this stretch on numerous occasions since, always with at least a modicum of success but have never encountered identical conditions nor such willing fish again. It was certainly a case of being in the right place at the right time and a vindication of blind fishing.

A backcountry river typified by pools rather than lengthy runs requires a totally different approach. If it is not possible to sight fish effectively then a very careful study of the current lines is essential. Such

Casting across a lateral shear plane towards the head of a pool can result in a short fly drift. Before casting, an angler needs to consider carefully the best angle of approach.

places frequently present major technical difficulties in the form of back eddies, turbulent rapids dropping abruptly from the pool above, very deep water and circular currents. I used to actually dislike these sorts of pools for I found that fish were often right on the bottom in deep water or positioned in places where it was nigh impossible to effect a drag free drift. However, I'm now somewhat less overawed by them and will always spend a bit of time fishing them even when no fish are obvious. Such pools often form where a bluff or high, steep bank occurs on one side. One technique which has proved effective many times is to cast a small dry fly or terrestrial pattern to within centimetres of the bluff on the far side. Large fish are often positioned just beneath the surface taking advantage of the narrow feed line which is created as the water follows the contours of the rock face. Often the only warning is a slight break in the surface as the trout's neb appears and quickly inhales the fly. A quick set of the wrist is often all that's required to hook-up.

Big, deep pools invariably harbour more fish than may be visible and I always give them some serious attention. A double nymph rig with a highly visible indicator well back from the flies can prove deadly when thrown right up into the fast water. Sometimes fish will be feeding actively in the fast water or deep below the drop-off. Vigilance and quick reactions are essential. I will strike at any hesitation, dip in the indicator or drawing under of the floating line. In this situation I will not be in any hurry to lift the line from the water and have been rewarded many times by a take when the fly line is well downstream of my casting position. The nymph has often been taken right on the bottom. Sometimes a single "bomb" or heavily weighted single nymph is the key.

Perhaps my favourite form of blind nymphing is fishing relatively shallow water just below a significant rapid at the head of a long, laminar flowing run. Some rivers lend themselves perfectly to this technique, none more so than the Motueka River at times. Whilst such places can frequently prove quite disappointing, when a good mayfly hatch is in progress they may liven up in spectacular fashion. I like to fish a long leader and tippet of at least four metres tapered down to 4 or preferably 5X. A single mayfly nymph imitation like a Pheasant Tail or Turkey Tail or a small Beadhead will usually suffice. Where the run drops off into deeper water over 60 centimetres or so deep I use a double nymph rig with one small but well weighted nymph such as a Tungsten Beadhead and a smaller, unweighted, more natural one such as a Pheasant Tail. When the fish are really active be prepared for surprises as some takes will come in water barely deep enough to support the bulk of a sizeable trout. If a number of fish are visible it is likely that others, unseen are lurking in the vicinity too. When the activity is intense it is possible to rest such an area after the fish have been disturbed and go back in after a decent interval of perhaps twenty minutes or so and catch yet more, as the urge to take advantage of the excellent meal on offer will override fear. Regrettably these situations don't occur frequently enough but its odds on that there will nearly always be a few fish feeding in such locations.

The real "hot-spot" of such runs is the shear line which separates the quiet water of the eye from the main current.

Brown trout in particular often favour this feeding niche more than any other, using the quieter water of the eye to rest in between brief forays out into the faster water to snatch food being washed down in the drift. Fishing these places calls for stealth and accurate casting. I frequently observe two major errors in fishing these locations. The first is to start fishing too far up the run, thereby scaring all the fish lower down, some of which at least may have been catchable. The correct technique is to begin well down the run and only progress upstream by miniscule increments. If I am confident that fish are present I will spend a great deal of time placing literally scores of casts through the likely water. I also subscribe to fishing to a pattern. Far too often I see anglers making their first cast right out into the middle of the stream, effectively lining any fish between the angler and the centre. It pays to begin close in and gradually fan the casts further and further out until satisfied that the area has been well covered. Only then will I move up and repeat the process. If I have a hunch that there are still fish to be had I'll even change the size or pattern of fly and try again. Of course extreme stealth and good technique is required along with a positive attitude. If one is convinced that feeding fish are present and takes the attitude that every cast has the potential to result in a hook-up success will come, even on slow days when not much is happening. If success does not come it is possibly time to have a good hard look at our equipment and the casting and mending technique being applied.

A blind fishing method which rarely seems to rate mention these days is fishing across and down. For some peculiar reason popular opinion is that this is a method reserved purely for fishing small, traditional wet flies in the dusk. This too is a highly effective method. When conditions were right I regularly caught a dozen or more fish in the hour before dark on the Motueka, particularly in the late summer when a big caddis hatch was on. But the nymph may also be fished in this fashion with confidence at any time of day. For a few years I guided in the Nelson One Fly Competition and on a number of occasions my team for the day came out on top purely because they fished their single nymphs across and down all day. My advice was simply to try to cover as much water, and therefore as many fish as possible. Fishing nymphs across and down is one of the most relaxing and simple angling methods I know, but is most suitable for larger rivers and long, even flowing runs. Unlike the traditional across and down method which was once so popular on big rivers like the Tongariro fishing a nymph in this style does not require a sinking line or shooting head. A floating, weight forward or sink tip line will suffice. During the brighter part of the day a leader of similar length to that which would be fished upstream is required, but this may be shortened considerably in the early morning or evening.

The technique involves casting across the current to a point a little upstream of the angler. This is important as the nymph needs time to get near the bottom. As soon as the line is on the water one should begin to apply small upstream mends in order that as much as possible a dead drift is achieved. These mends usually only require a flick of the wrist, just enough to prevent a belly of line forming. As soon as a belly forms in the floating line the nymph is accelerated unnaturally and the object is to achieve a natural drift. As the line progresses down the current follow the approximate position of the nymph with the rod tip with the rod held parallel to the water surface and some loose line held in the non-rod hand. If a take is to occur it is most likely to happen just as the fly reaches the end of its drift and begins to swing towards the bank. I suspect that at this point the nymph begins to move up in the water column and is taken by any fish which may be in the vicinity fearing that its prey is about to escape. There is no need for an indicator as the take is normally registered with a solid pull. Striking hard is totally unnecessary and may actually result in a break-off as the fish hits the fly heading downstream. A gentle lift and tightening will suffice as normally the fish is well hooked or simply comes off straightaway. While this tends to fool a lot of smaller fish it will work on larger ones too, especially when the river is dropping after a fresh. It is a technique I frequently use to introduce beginners to fly fishing or if the wind is simply too strong to fish directly upstream. The ideal situation is a moderate upstream breeze. Over the years it has proven a highly effective method, accounting for many excellent fish. In the evening a small wet fly such as a Purple Grouse may be substituted for a nymph, or else use an unweighted nymph.

In the ideal world we would spend every minute of each outing fishing to trout which have been spotted first. Indeed, on some rare occasions this is the norm. I have only to think of some of the smaller backcountry gems of north-west Nelson and the West Coast in the right conditions and recall some amazing days when every fish was seen first. Realistically conditions are very seldom so perfect and at best we must utilise a combination of these techniques. The exact percentage of the mix will vary enormously from stream to stream and from day to day. Blind fishing is not just "chuck and chance" as some would describe it. The term is very much a misnomer. The more skilful one becomes the more this will become apparent.

Chapter 10 : Trophy Hunting

During nearly fifty years of angling I have witnessed many titanic battles between fishermen and trout. I can recall one fish I hooked on the Borland River that took fifty-seven minutes to land. Another brown, on the West Coast, assisted by the power of a swollen river, sped off downstream stripping all of the fly line from my reel in a matter of seconds. But it did not stop there — not at all — it pushed on and on, taking my backing as well. Eventually there was none of that left either and only a tiny knot linked angler and fish. Remarkably the trout came to rest at that point. After negotiating endless obstacles I gradually retrieved all of the line and eventually netted the fish! Many struggles emerge in my memory, however, few match the duel that I saw John Cornish engage in last season.

We were fishing on one of those rivers that regularly produces very large trout — fish of 3.5 kilograms, 4.5 kilograms and 5 or 6 kilograms if one is really lucky. I was sneaking among the undergrowth that clothed a high bank, overlooking a substantial pool. I was the spotter. John scrambled along a boulder-strewn shore, staying back a little, awaiting and no doubt hoping for my call, "See one!"

Towards the head of the pool, a huge, submerged rock rose from the river bed. Trout are attracted to flow obstructions like this. So are my eyes when I'm stalking. The trout that lay ahead of the boulder, despite being on the bed in about three metres of water, was plain to see. I uttered the words John desired, but added, "He's huge!" No doubt John hoped for that too! I was tempted to venture, "My turn!" — but refrained.

Always expectant and hopeful, John endeavoured to lift the fish to the surface with a bushy dry fly. "Ambitious," I quipped, timing the comment to follow the failure. The fish did not even acknowledge that the fly had passed over its head. Next John tried a weighted nymph. Despite the drop being well ahead of target I suspected that the nymph had drifted too high. It was not inspected either. "More weight needed," I ventured, again after the offering had been ignored.

Next John added a second, heavier nymph to his tippet then flung it upstream. I'm certain his head jerked left as the nymphs sped past. They hit the water with a splooosh rather than a plop — in a manner that suggested they would sink quickly. Even so, the fish still lifted a surprising distance to intercept. John's tiny, yarn indicator dipped. His rod tip whipped skywards, the battle was on.

From my vantage point I could watch angler and fish and survey their battlefield with ease. Upstream stood a deep gorge. Thirty metre bluffs confined the river on either side. Downstream the pool was more open but deep and six or seven hundred metres long. That's the direction the fish took. It dived back to the bed then sped for the far shore, fleeing its foe. Then it bore back upstream. The strong current and "heavy water" seemed no burden whatsoever — another hint that this was a really big trout. It continued up for some distance then, for no apparent reason, turned and sped towards John, came almost to his feet. This was a fish with enormous energy and an equally large will to eliminate the burden it had so suddenly acquired.

Meanwhile, John just clung to his rod (which he had thrust high in the air to free as much line from the water as possible) and at first allowed the fish all the line it desired — then he reeled in hastily when the fish approached at speed. I sensed his relief when contact was regained after the slack was taken up. For a brief moment the fish appeared less desperate. For a short time it sneaked along the nearby bed, a sluggish, immoveable weight. Then it was away once more, out into the fast current and downstream. This time it was not a panic stricken run but one of steady resolve. The ten metres that had separated fish and angler soon became twenty, then thirty. It was time for John to move — and fast.

I watched anxiously but in awe — in awe of the power of the fish, concerned about John's slow and perilous progress over a jumble of slimy rocks separated by pockets of deep water. The distance between fish and angler grew steadily and a new hazard loomed. A huge boulder rose from the water mid-stream, one that the fish was certain to pass on the outside. It did. John's burdens became three: The weight of the monster, an ever increasing length of line (and its weight and drag in the water) and the line hooked and scraping around the rock. John plunged towards the rock, waist-deep in the water flicking his rod tip upwards as he went. The line sprang free, however, in the meantime it had been wrapped around two more boulders downstream. The fish pushed on relentlessly. John, well adrift, jaw pushed forward, followed — motivated by a thread of hope that the fish would falter soon, waver in its resolve.

By the time that John had freed the line from behind a third rock I was at his side. He had regained some "ground" but the join between fly line and backing was still far away in the current. While John did close a little on the fish we could both see that the battle was soon to end — not

A very large trout being carried to the shore, secure in a net.

with the fish held aloft in the net or slipped gradually up a sandy shore but with it disappearing down a boisterous, deep rapid negotiable by fish alone. As the fish was drawn down into the rapid its pace quickened then the tippet broke. John's rod became suddenly lifeless. His left hand, still holding the net, moved to his hip.

His bottom lip pushed out a little. Then he became as lifeless as his rod — a figure staring at where the fish had been. When reality reluctantly returned we spoke. Our estimates of the fish's weight began to climb. As we shall discuss later, John felt that he was never really in control.

Obviously we'll never know whether the fish was a trophy (4.5kg or more) but it was indisputably very big. Our memory of it is equally grand. The fact that the fish was lost is not entirely surprising. In fact I'd venture to suggest that there are more really big fish lost than caught. Most evade anglers even before a fly is cast — they hear heavy footfalls or spot anglers lurking above the water. Poorly selected or presented flies alert many trophy fish too while many of those that err and are stung by a hook escape an angler by breaking his line with their power or throw the hook during a prolonged fight. Because the odds favour trophy fish and not anglers it is important, if we wish to prevail occasionally, that we learn what we can about these rare prizes and use that knowledge where we can.

What follows is largely a summary of my observations of big trout as they fed and responded to the anglers who sought to deceive them or land them when hooked. I've been fortunate to witness about thirty five trophy trout come to shore and seen more than that number escape after they had been hooked — statistically not a huge sample but significant enough experience to share.

Where The Trophies Choose To Dine

Historically, trophy trout were found in most rivers and streams in New Zealand. For example I have an old photo, somewhere in my collection, of a seven kilogram brown caught in the 1930s in the tiny Waiwera Stream, in South Otago. I doubt that there has been a similar fish there for several decades. Hosts of other streams would have yielded their own monsters at about the same time. Nowadays there are still some big ones to be chased but their distribution is somewhat more confined, it seems, to particular waters.

Some trout rivers are trophy waters and some are not. Why this is so can be only partially explained. What is known is that for trout to reach trophy proportions they need to grow quite quickly. They require a rich food supply and to feed in waters at an appropriate temperature for maximum benefit to be gained from it. Their food should be gathered with minimal energy cost and they need to delay their first reproductive activity for perhaps two years. In addition the ability for the fish to migrate downstream from headwaters to an estuary or the ocean where food is plentiful is probably very important too.

Sometimes abnormal conditions can contribute to some fish reaching giant proportions rapidly — such as during a beech tree mast year. This event leads to an explosion in the population of mice which feed on beech nuts and in turn provides a very healthy and fattening food supply for trout.

While we understand these things there is far more that we do not know especially about population dynamics in particular river systems — feeding conditions, food availability, temperature regimes, the age distribution of fish, migration habits and so on. Hopefully some of these secrets will be revealed to the curious in time.

Where I fish, in the South Island, there is a broad pattern to the location of trophy waters. First, the estuaries and tidal zones of many rivers on both sides of the island support big trout, particularly in the spring and early summer. The location and size of these fish can be explained. They are attracted by an abundant food supply — whitebait, smelt and other small fish — and fatten quickly.

The inland waters that regularly support really big fish tend to be east of the main divide although there are one or two rivers with plenty of trophies in the west too. It is interesting to note that some "trophy rivers" do not have an equal distribution of big fish along their length. Some sections hold trophies yet other parts have predominantly smaller fish.

Similarly, within some large river systems some tributaries are trophy waters while others, even neighbouring ones, are not. And here is an interesting thing. I have fished neighbouring waters like this and frequently thought that the "non-trophy waters" looked healthier and more stable than those producing big fish. The non-trophy rivers have mostly held greater numbers of trout.

The inland trophy waters are not necessarily the most remote rivers. They do tend to be rivers that are connected to a large waterway. This would hint at the importance of some migration particularly in the long term maintenance of stock. However, I have noticed, after visiting some trophy waters regularly, that many big fish are strongly territorial and do not stray from one place or even from an exact feeding lie but remain there not just for weeks on end but for several seasons running. This, however, does not exclude the possibility of migration for part of a year. I have seen many more trophy jack fish than hen fish. This could suggest that some hen fish are more migratory than their early winter mates. Also the inland trophy rivers are usually rivers with small numbers of trout per kilometre. In these rivers I have not caught many smaller fish (one to two kilograms).

Big trout water in spring. A river (east of the divide) rather than a stream — with spacious deep pools.

This could suggest that this age group has migrated downstream to feed. The bigger resident fish may be trout that have returned following their migration.

Feeding Behaviours Of Big Trout

Exploring new waters is always exciting for an angler. Each new pool promises the excitement of the unknown and new lessons to be learned. However, there is an equal amount to be gleaned from repeated visits to a river. I have returned to several "trophy rivers" annually and noted some patterns about the whereabouts of the big fish and the feeding behaviour that they exhibit.

Big fish tend to like being in or near to big water. By that I mean pools that have both considerable width and a depth of several metres. In addition, trophy trout seek pools that have some stability to the bed — a substantial section of bedrock or an extensive area of large, immoveable boulders. These pools usually have at least one stable shore and a bank that is well vegetated. A section of the bed will be vegetated too, with algae and other aquatic plants. Beds like this are favoured by the aquatic insects that nourish trout.

Really big trout do not tend to dwell in pocket water, unless it is along the margins of a pool. They will not usually be found in shallow water either. In fact the majority of trophy trout hug close to the bed in the stomach of the pool they occupy. And most feed there (on drifting invertebrates) and will not be tempted to lift very far.

In the summer, however, when there is profit to be gained from an abundance of surface food, some monstrous fish will hold higher in the water and rise. But often these fish will hover further below the surface (maybe a metre or so down) than more impetuous, smaller relatives.

Often really big trout will not hold in one spot for a long period. I've noticed that some of them will feed in a particular lie but then drift downstream for no apparent reason — then they may feed in a new location or eventually return to the original lie. Other big ones may feed in an area rather than a particular lie. They patrol their territory constantly feeding as they move.

Trophy sized trout can be very selective feeders. They would not have survived to reach giant proportions if they had not been discerning, hence I have always believed that an angler has his best chance of snaring a trout on his first cast. With each drop thereafter the chances diminish.

This is probably even more significant when fishing to a really big fish. This leads to a tip about fishing to a big one that proves elusive. The lesson was reinforced by my friend Smithy last season. Smithy found a "grandad of a fish" feeding very close to the shore. I knew, from my vantage point on the other side of the river that it was a really big fish. Smithy's forward lean was more pronounced than usual, his stoop a little lower and when he cast his grip with both hands was rigid. He was ready to strike! However, despite a fine range of flies and nymphs being offered not one suited the taste of the fish. Smithy could have continued to probe as long as the fish continued to show interest.

Instead he sneaked away and left the fish undisturbed for an hour or more. Interestingly when he returned he hooked the fish on his first cast. Unfortunately it was another of those that got away — but not before demonstrating its immense power. As with John's fish described earlier, Smithy never felt in control. The lesson for me was that if a big fish does prove elusive then sometimes it is better to stop fishing to it for a while and then try again later.

Probably the sooner an angler stops the greater the chances of later success. Big trout do display some signals that indicate when it is time to let them rest. The first sign is a subtle change in their feeding behaviour. They may intercept food less frequently or cease ranging as far for nymphs. They may decline surface food that was being taken previously. Sometimes their motion may appear less fluid, and their body appear more rigid. They may

Another potential trophy water with deep pools stabilised by large boulders providing plenty of cover for trout but also harbouring abundant aquatic trout food.

sink closer to the river bed or change their position completely — move upstream or drift back a little. A trout that displays one or several of these changes is a more wary fish, alerted and suspicious — but not necessarily alarmed.

Big fish that are alarmed will usually move quite distinctly away from where they feed — usually to the sanctuary of deep water. Normally they will not bolt like their smaller offspring but drift gradually from view. It is rare to catch a trout soon after it has been alarmed. If there is truth in the assertion that the first cast to a fish is the one that is most likely to bring it to a "fly" then it makes sense to maximise the effectiveness of that cast — especially when a fat, and undoubtedly fussy specimen lies ahead. Special thought and care should be given when preparing to cast to a big one. An angler should endeavour to probe to the fish's depth immediately with a sensible choice of "fly" — both in pattern and size. The increased excitement and expectation (compounded by reminders of the fish's size by fishing partners!) can make the first cast to a large fish even more challenging than usual.

An angler holding a firm-fleshed, young trophy jack-fish. Note that there is little body or belly sag over the angler's hand. The fish is relatively short, its head is small, the back humped with tight skin covering the body.

Some Features Of Trophy Trout

Four and a half kilogram trout are almost invariably very healthy fish. They are usually 68–72 centimetres long, are thick across the shoulders and just forward of the caudal fin and they possess a belly. Some will even be slightly humped behind their head. Younger trophy trout are very firm. Slightly older ones can be "a little" softer to touch, especially in the belly.

When a trout is in the water it is difficult to be certain about its exact size. Surprisingly, one can be most deceived making estimates in the clearest waters. A trout's length is often reasonably apparent when the fish is in the water but what is less obvious are the real dimensions that determine whether a fish is really heavy — the shoulder and back width and belly depth. Colour is quite important. Usually when I am fishing to a dark fish I hold little hope that it will be a trophy. Fat, healthy trout tend to look paler in the water.

The size of trout is frequently over-estimated by anglers looking directly down on them. This was emphasised to me recently — and not for the first time. My brother, Ho, and I visited a river which flowed through private property in a remote valley. When we sought permission for access from the farmer he told us furtively and in a hushed voice about "a ten pounder" that fed daily at the foot of a very steep bank. In the afternoon Ho and I found the "ten pounder." We looked down on it from the top of a thirty metre drop and were impressed by what we saw — immediately eager to test its mettle.

Ho descended to the river and positioned himself downstream from the fish. I watched from above. My bank-top position gave me a marvellous view of trout and angler. Ho's initial cast rose the fish. It sped for the nearest deep water when hooked. However, the battle was not prolonged and the "ten pounder" was in fact about half that size. It lacked depth, it lacked width and had not quite the length of a prize fish. It had looked more impressive in the water than out. Ho put it back, perhaps with some hope that it would be a real trophy in a year or two.

Battling A Big One

The principles of playing trout are similar no matter what the size of the fish, and Graeme has discussed these in detail. However, trophy sized trout behave in some different ways than smaller specimens and their immense power must always be respected and considered.

Really big trout almost invariably react with tremendous force when first hooked. They rarely leap clear of the water, instead they usually dive deep. Their first run is normally very robust, prolonged and unimpeded even if it is upstream into a fast flow. During this energetic onslaught it is best to avoid pressuring the fish in any way — it should be allowed to run freely. However, an angler has to be wary of the increasing length of line being pulled into the water. This line and the pressure of the current on it is increasing the burden on the tippet. This is particularly so when the fish has sped across the river causing a belly in the line. There can be several responses at this time (with the ultimate aim of shortening the length of line between angler and the fish). First, the fish should be followed as much as is possible and at the same time the rod raised skywards at arm's length to lift as much line as possible clear of the water. Then, when the run has slowed or ceased any belly in the line should be eased from the water so that the angler has a straight line to the prize. It is reasonable to suggest that if an angler still has contact with the fish after the initial flurry and has established the shortest possible, direct line with it, then the chances of bringing it to land will have increased immeasurably.

Often after their first run, really big trout will become dogged. They will patrol along the bed (usually out of sight) upstream and down — an immoveable, nose-down, deadweight. There is little an angler can do but follow — keeping the line as short as possible. But they must also remain alert, ready for another burst of energy from the fish, ready to yield immediately. Again this is a time when little pressure should be exerted. The fish still has too much energy. Patience is the key to success at this stage of the battle.

After a considerable time, and gradually increased pressure from the angler, the fish will begin to yield and can be coaxed little by little towards shallower water. Often the gains that an angler makes will be countered by another run. These should not be opposed. The landing of a trophy trout is probably the dream of most anglers. When one is finally hooked an angler can become very eager to complete the task quickly. The short route is to be patient, be wary and respect the fish that has finally been hooked. Any belief that the battle has been won before the fish lies on its side is a dangerous one. Any thought that the struggle will be brief is misplaced.

I believe that it is better to beach a large trout than to meet it with a net. Usually beaching is easier near to the tail of a pool where the bed gradient is gradual and bed material finer. I prefer to "play the fish with my feet" rather than from the reel — this means walking backwards, coaxing it into shallow water. As long as the fish keeps coming the angler should continue backing away. The time to retrieve line on the reel is when no further progress is being made or when the fish topples onto its side. No

matter how shallow the water may be, if a trout remains upright it can still escape at high speed, especially a very large trout. While a trout is being eased shorewards it will continually try to turn its nose back out into the river. Each turn can be countered gently, with pressure in the opposite direction. But if the fish decides to turn and run, and it probably will at some stage, it should not be hindered.

With patience, some persuasion and a little luck the fish will eventually fall over onto its side in the shallows. Only then is it safe to move with haste. Only then is it safe to think, "He's mine!"

While the principles of landing all trout may be similar there is an idea related to size that is important to remember always. The notion is that as the size of trout increases then the control balance changes from angler to fish. When an angler hooks a fish of less than a kilogram weight they can almost reel it in at will. A one to one and a half kilogram fish will succumb relatively quickly too after an initial flurry. The angler will nearly always be in charge. However, when a trout in the two to three kilogram range is hooked then there is a considerable time during which the fish has to be "given its head." I believe that a trophy trout, when hooked is almost totally in control. With this belief arises respect. Respect will strengthen the chances of success, improve the odds of completing a victorious trophy hunt.

An angler endeavouring to beach a large trout. Note that the bed where the fish is being pulled ashore is devoid of large stones (potential obstructions) so the fish can be coaxed ashore smoothly. The gentle slope is helpful in this respect too.

Chapter 11 : To Stalk
Or Not To Stalk?

We are all well aware of the convolutions and apparent inconsistencies of the English language. Indeed, I never cease to be amazed that mastery of it can be achieved by those whose first language is not English. The Concise Oxford Dictionary lists three totally different and distinct meanings for the word 'stalk'. It is common knowledge that plants have stalks but it is rather curious that one definition – to "stride, walk in a stately or imposing manner," is so very different and almost directly opposite in meaning from the one which is the cornerstone of this book, that is, to "steal up to game under cover; pursue stealthily." The act of stalking wild animals is familiar and conjures up images of a deerstalker glassing a windswept, Scottish corrie in search of magnificent red deer stags, or of an intrepid hunter pushing through dense jungle foliage somewhere in darkest equatorial Africa while his native guides deferentially follow on behind. But stalking fish – and a single fish at that has not really formed a major part of our angling culture or literature despite the fact that fishers have been stalking since time immemorial. The African fisherman standing in rigid pose in a shallow lake with spear poised ready to drive into the flank of a fat carp is stalking in the purest sense. So too is the angler stealthily parting the bullrushes on the edge of an English chalk stream searching for the tell-tale rise form of a fine brown trout. Try telling the fisher wading the shallow, sun-drenched flats of Christmas Island in search of bonefish and permit that what he is doing is not stalking. The practice is far from novel but we need to examine its implications for trout fishers.

To do this we also need to explore the meaning of the term for us. The authors perceive stalking primarily as an act which will, hopefully, enable us to see a trout before it is aware of our presence. From experience we have discovered that a trout which is aware of an angler is immediately more difficult, and in some cases impossible to catch. In chapter 8 though, I recounted the story of an Italian angler who succeeded in taking a large brown from a deep pool in a back country river. I mentioned that I felt convinced that the fish were fully aware of our presence but due to the

Opposite page: A bouldery back country river with plenty of likely trout lies evident.

depth at which they were holding felt secure and safe from predators there.

We stalk mainly to see before being seen or detected in some way. This does not necessarily mean that we absolutely must see every potential target. Far from it. But precedents have taught us that an undisturbed fish is an infinitely more attractive target than one which has been alerted. Therefore it is simply good form to use techniques which optimise any given opportunity. Each situation must be taken on its merits. A deep, murky river typical of many of our larger waterways in their lower reaches requires little application of stealth to fish effectively. Spinning equipment, streamer flies cast with heavy sinking lines and short, stout leaders are likely to achieve the desired result. But switch locations to the middle reaches of the Motueka say on a bright January day. Imagine a typically long run, perhaps 200 or more metres long. We are stalking up the true left bank as the other side is overhung by willows and access is impossible. Forced to the open, shallow side we feel totally exposed as progress upstream is via a broad expanse of cobblestone sized boulders and there simply is no cover. There is no obvious sign of a significant hatch taking place. Just an occasional caddis fly and an even rarer mayfly flutter over the surface of the water. Inviting though the sparkling surface water may seem a glance into the river aided by polarised lenses reveals an almost uniform coating of brown algae on the rocks. Not a fish is in sight.

These conditions are totally daunting to many but familiarity with one's water spawns confidence for it is a situation like this which I revel in. Indeed, I've sometimes spent the bulk of a three or four hour session on just one typical stretch, and with wonderful results. Here is where the stalking method becomes the only practical one. The need for stealth simply cannot be stressed enough. If they have been undisturbed for some time brown trout will often be found in extremely shallow water. This is where correctly set-up equipment is vital. My ideal choice would be for a weight 4 or 5 rod with double taper or weight forward floating line combination. The flyline must be of neutral colour. I favour olive green, brown or tan in that order. The leader will need to be long and the tippet relatively fine – in the region of 1.5 – 2kg breaking strain. When actively stalking individual fish in shallow water I will use a single, lightly weighted nymph and the smallest indicator which is still visible, or dispense with this altogether and tie a highly visible parachute hackled dry fly on a dropper. Sometimes I choose to fish with a small (#16) dry fly on its own, for even though no rises may be seen a trout feeding in shallow water will rarely pass up on such an offering.

This is a time to pause and take stock. Rivers like this carry fish in numbers. On any given summer day, providing that the barometer is not plunging a significant proportion will be available to the angler. Many more will undoubtedly be feeding in deep, mid-stream water (where they are still catchable). The remainder, and who knows how many that may be, will be holed up amongst the ever protective willows clothing the faraway bank.

Sight fishing in open water on a low country stream like the Motueka is infinitely more difficult than doing so on a bouldery back country one.

The latter has far more features to provide clues to the whereabouts of trout in the form of distinct pockets, bank extensions and protruding boulders. The former requires intense concentration, skill and a positive attitude. Inevitably some fish will be scared. Each time this happens a lesson should be learned. One needs to ask just why the trout was positioned in that location. Perhaps there was a slight depression in the streambed. Maybe it found refuge of a sort in front of a larger rock than the average for the stretch. It may have found a niche in a pocket of quiet water adjacent to the main current. While the stretch may seem totally featureless initially, this is rarely the case. Slowly but surely the puzzle should begin to unravel and all being equal an unsuspecting fish should be encountered before too long. Perhaps you are suddenly aware of a trout weaving gently in the current. How did you miss seeing it sooner you ask yourself. At this point careful observation is essential. Try to work out the feeding pattern and how active the fish is. If possible back off carefully as a cast from a really close position would probably result in a spooked fish.

All movements must be unhurried. Question if the rig is suitable for the situation. Is the nymph too heavy? Would a dry fly be worth trying first? Try to keep the fish within your window of observation. Sometimes this may require a lateral movement. Make a decision on the side to cast to or from. Is line shadow likely to prove problematic? There are many decisions to be made once a fish is in sight. Many anglers are intimidated by rivers such as this but they needn't be. A common myth is that the fish there are incredibly spooky – not so, or at least not significantly more so than in many other rivers. But these trout have seen anglers before and know exactly how to respond if there is the slightest hint of threat. Shallow waters are dangerous places for trout and they are fully aware of it. But if food in sufficient quantity is available trout, especially browns will be there.

Fishing to large trout in shallow water is incredibly exciting when every movement of the fish can be observed. Most anglers will admit to a quickening of the pulse when there is a fish in sight. A favourite former client of mine used to comment on this situation sagely, "You know Graeme, at

An angler casting into the top section of a run. The bed has numerous large boulders making it a most likely place for several trout to feed.

some point the cast has to be made," and I would see him literally steeling himself to attempt to make the perfect one. Gary is a highly intelligent man with both a legal and science background and I suspect that very little that he does in life, including fly fishing is left to chance. I never had to stress the importance of the first cast with him. His clinical approach to the problem ensured that he enjoyed great success. He was a dream to guide, as he was a superb caster and equally adept with either hand, meaning that he could target fish in situations which would be difficult for the average angler. The only chink in his armour, so to speak, was the aforementioned nervousness when confronted by the challenge of making that first cast. In a few weaker moments he admitted to being subject to a serious case of nerves when he had a large New Zealand trout just metres away. I constantly reassured him by asserting strongly that he was not alone. I still have to take a grip of myself when I come across a big fish feeding actively.

We have discussed at some length the difference between truly fishing blind and fishing blind with conviction and method. The latter should be very much part of every angler's repertoire. Even though a fish may not actually be in sight we need to calculate where one might be. Correct technique and a methodical, thinking approach will produce results. Back to the Motueka again. Much of this fine river is impossible to see into even on a bright, sunny day with little or no wind. It is a relatively large river throughout much of its length and on some days the fish are simply not to be found in the shallow edges where they can be sighted and cast to individually. I referred earlier to the mid-stream area. Even if little insect activity is apparent I will fish this deeper, usually faster water, especially in the top 25% of any given run with real conviction.

If the run has some obvious larger structure in the form of boulders or rock outcroppings I become even more interested. This is the place for a long leader, two small but well weighted nymphs and a highly visible indicator. If the surface is quite broken, or "joggly" so much the better. I will rarely walk past such places without giving them some serious attention as they can prove to be real treasure troves. Research has proved that this is often the most productive part of any given run.

The technique is relatively simple requiring a long, drag free drift through likely water. I always have a hard look at the water before commencing. Big water is daunting, so it is necessary to mentally break it up into smaller streams. Throwing one cast thoughtlessly right out into the middle, followed immediately by one directly upstream close to the bank is pointless and comes into the category of fishing randomly – definitely not a stalking technique. I am rarely content with just one drift through high probability water. One has only to observe how many times a nymph will pass by a fish which has been sighted sometimes before it finally attracts the fish's attention and is taken to realise that when fishing blind many fish are simply passed over due to a lack of patience on the part of the angler. It is crucial to fish to a pattern. Normally I advocate starting close in to the shore and proceed by 'fanning ' casts out further and further into the central part of the stream. Sometimes a fish will not deviate from its feed line by more than a few centimetres so it needs opportunities to see the fly within its self proscribed feed-line.

Patience and perseverance are indeed virtues. I had an experience which confirmed this for me on the Motueka near the Wangapeka confluence one day. It was late in the afternoon and the light was very poor for sight fishing as the sky had gradually clouded over throughout the day. I'd had a successful outing all the same and had determined to just fish out this particular run before commencing the long trudge back to my vehicle. Towards the top the visibility improved markedly as a small bluff towered up on the other side, effectively cutting out much of the surface reflection. The water was quite deep and I could see a couple of fish on the bottom in a metre and a half or so of water. My attempts to hook both proved unsuccessful and, somewhat disgusted with my performance I very nearly called it a day right then as the top of the run was close. The bulk of the river's flow rushed swiftly over a distinct drop-off and was very narrow at this point. Normally I would not have given this place more than a cursory glance and a few half-hearted casts to the edge of the white water but something encouraged me to treat it with less disdain this time. My first cast landed right along the seam between the boiling rapid and the very insignificant eye. I became even more interested when I sensed rather than saw a flash of silver as a fish slashed at and missed the nymph. A couple of careful casts produced no response and then suddenly there it was. I hardly saw the indicator dip but instinct prevailed and when I lifted the rod I was firmly attached to a solid fish which cartwheeled down the rapid and into the body of the run. Some minutes later I subdued and released a nicely conditioned hen of about 1.8kg. Amazingly I was to repeat the performance three more times. The fish must have been almost climbing over the top of one another as the area of possible holding water was miniscule, perhaps a couple of square metres at most. Interestingly the normally tedious trudge back to the vehicle was a breeze. I could very easily have dismissed this little holding area as being too insignificant.

Fishing to a previously spotted fish is simply great fun, and as explained, despite having observed literally thousands of fish over the years I still experience a little thrill when I'm successful in locating one which hasn't already seen me. As a guide there have been times when I simply couldn't resist moving on ahead to the next likely stretch of water. One of my clients was quite content to amble quietly along, taking care not to slip and fall on the boulders as he knew that I would never walk past a fish that was even vaguely catchable.

"Just like a setter on point," was how he described me when it was obvious that I had a fish in view. "All I have to do is wander up and Graeme will have it pin-pointed for me."

As much as most (but not all) anglers prefer sight fishing, pragmatism dictates that a considerable part of most outings will be spent employing some form of blind fishing technique, but more of that later. Some seemingly inauspicious days can produce surprisingly good conditions for sight fishing. This is where selection of water can become critical. Wide open, relatively featureless rivers can be very hard to fish or to stalk on dull, windy days. Bankside vegetation and high banks or bluffs can sometimes assist by cutting surface reflection, and pockets between willows, for example, can provide respite from even quite vicious winds. While grey or even rainy days make life difficult on wide valley floors they can enhance prospects in steep-sided, relatively narrow valleys. I actually prefer total cloud cover, even steady rain to bright sunny conditions, or worse, intermittent sun and cloud, particularly early and late in the season when the sun is low in the sky. My pet hate is a situation of part sun, part shade as its almost impossible to see into shade from the sunny side and fish are easily scared by the angler standing out starkly. Spotting is much easier from the shadow but the benefits can be negated by reflection off bluffs, edges of terraces or even vegetation. Extra caution is required but some of the best fishing days I have ever experienced have occurred on some of the dullest imaginable with mist almost right down to the valley floor, or in heavy rain where the patter of raindrops on the surface can actually aid and abet the angler.

Les and I were extremely fortunate to have experienced what can rightly be described as "champagne" fishing before the advent of helicopter aided fishing in many back country areas of the South Island. In retrospect we probably did not fully appreciate the quality of these experiences in light of today's angling pressure. These wild, beautiful and once rarely visited places have since become the mecca of anglers from all over the world. This became particularly apparent to me when I became a professional fishing guide myself. During more than a decade of guiding on the rivers of Kahurangi National Park I became very aware of the effects of angling pressure. I quickly found that the optimum time to fish there was immediately following a significant flood when the fish responded to the extra food on offer and showed relatively little fear. The times I began to dread were towards the end of a long stretch of very settled weather, especially when water levels became very low. On some days it was difficult to catch a single fish, and though I could probably count them on the fingers of one hand I experienced a few totally blank days. On those days the fish simply didn't show themselves or else fled at the first cast. However, I did come up with a few strategies which quite often worked. If another party of anglers had been through the water even a day or so earlier very few fish would be out feeding in places where they could normally be relied upon. Despite perfect spotting conditions the fish simply could not be found. The few which ventured out were frequently quite uneasy and ready to quit feeding at the slightest hint of danger.

I'm convinced that a large percentage of brown trout become nocturnal feeders when under intense pressure. Others retreat to places less accessible to anglers. Drift divers have reported seeing fish, apparently in resting mode, curled neatly around large rocks. Others seek sanctuary under banks, amongst flood debris, and alongside and under submerged logs. Some go to deep water and hug the bottom there, but just a few continue to feed, albeit in deep, fast water or in the midst of relatively shallow, swift water.

These latter places are normally far too inhospitable at times of normal flow but as water velocity decreases habitable pockets begin to appear and trout will use these places to feed.

I quickly adapted my angling strategies to cope with the ever changing circumstances I was faced with, and after a while knew precisely which part of my favourite beats were worth targeting. When the going got really tough there was simply no option but to fish the water blind. Tungsten beadhead nymphs are to me one of the most important innovations in modern fly fishing because of the superior weight to bulk ratio over the old style beads used in nymph construction. I actually proved this to my co-author on a Westland river a couple of Easters ago. We found ourselves fishing water which had been literally thrashed over the preceding days by a group of spin fishers camped nearby so we were under no illusion about the difficulty we faced. However, it was new water for me so we decided to do a little exploring anyway.

Initially we leap-frogged each other fishing blind into the lovely drop-offs which characterised the stream. We were not surprised to find a paucity of fish out feeding despite excellent spotting conditions considering the pressure which had been on the place over the long weekend. As expected the fishing was slow but I was thoroughly enjoying the sheer beauty of the location and the pleasure of laying out a long line, working the riffles, drop-offs and the deeper, very fishy looking water under the overhanging bush on the far side. Les fished carefully up through the top 25% or so of

a long run, concentrating especially on the near perfect drop-off at the top. He leaned forward expectantly and I was convinced that he would connect with a fish at any moment, but the tense pose slowly uncoiled and Les relaxed visibly, adopting a more upright stance.

A cast being made into the edge of deep fast water, the type of water that trout may retreat to during mid summer

"Nothing doing there," he uttered casually.

"I'll have a few casts, I replied. "You might have missed one, though I doubt it."

Les stood off to the side and watched as I set about fishing essentially the same water, prospecting my way methodically across the drop-off. I was on the point of winding in and proceeding up to the next run when the indicator stopped abruptly. I was quick enough to react and set the hook. A nice brown erupted from the tannin-stained water and just as quickly threw the hook. Somewhat amused we had a bit of a laugh about it and moved on. Les, as always generous when we fish together, invited me to have first shot, but I refused as I'd had a hook-up. Somewhat reluctantly he proceeded to adopt his serious fishing posture and carefully fished through the run, an almost carbon copy of the previous one. Once more, he had no joy.

"All right, let's see you do it again," he challenged.

"Why not," I replied cheekily and was flabbergasted when I hooked up within moments. This time the fish stayed attached and Les netted a lovely, golden-bellied jack.

"What are you using," he enquired as for the first time he took a long hard look at what was on the business end of my leader.

"Hell they're small," he commented examining the pair of #16 Tungsten Beadheads. They certainly made Les' #12 nymph look huge. I couldn't help but notice the somewhat covetous look in his eyes when I pulled out a small box full of tiny beadheads. My offer of a couple was politely declined.

We both touched nothing in the next couple of runs but there was one more stretch worth serious attention before we were back alongside the four wheel drive. History has a habit of repeating itself, and when I achieved another hook-up on a really nice fish which took me the best part of twenty minutes to land Tungsten Beadheads had another fan.

Part of the fascination of fly fishing lies in the difficulty factor and the sense of achievement gained when a particular problem is solved, if only for that moment. The variables associated with fly fishing alter so frequently that no two days, even on the same stretch of water, will ever be quite the same. We could spend our entire waking lives trying to outwit trout but still be nowhere near solving many of the mysteries which make them such alluring quarry.

In this chapter I have attempted to weigh up the arguments for and against the stalking method, which in the main implies sight fishing to us. Our perception of stalking is that it is a highly visual experience. Just as the big game hunter experiences a thrill when his patient glassing of rugged terrain results in the sighting of a deer, or perhaps a tahr or chamois, so too does the angler's pulse quicken when careful scrutiny reveals a fine trout holding station in a position where it can engulf the largest possible quantity of invertebrates as they tumble down in the current. To then complete the cast, induce the fish to take an artificial fly and hook it is a very special moment. The playing and landing may even enter the realms of anti-climax compared to the moment of the actual take. Other methods – wet fly, streamer fishing or even spin fishing all have their place and provide excitement and satisfaction enough but nothing can quite match the visual appeal of truly stalking.

Conclusion : Chance Or Choice?

It is no accident that serious fly fishers are also frequently very accomplished hunters as well. New Zealanders as a group have a passion for the outdoors, arguably second to none. Considering the superb natural playground which we have access to it is little wonder that this is so. Many Australians with a penchant for fishing and hunting envy us for our great variety of terrain and the ease of access to it. Trout fishing is often just one of the pursuits which outdoors orientated Kiwis indulge in along with hunting, tramping, diving, sea fishing, whitebaiting and a host of other activities. Hunters and fishers have a lot in common. To be successful in both areas requires meticulous preparation and planning, a love of wild places, keen observational skills and an ability to stalk.

Just as there are some really accomplished hunters there are also very proficient anglers. We may ask just what it is which enables some hunters to achieve at a higher level than others. For a start they plan — perhaps by talking with others who have visited an area before but also by perusing maps and aerial photos. They may have read articles about certain places, and will almost certainly check out access and routes. Efficient hunters are meticulous about their equipment. There is no point in owning a $2000 rifle if it is not sighted in correctly. Those who operate randomly without doing the homework may enjoy a modicum of success by sheer luck. But lucky hunters, just like lucky anglers may find that their successful forays are few and far between.

Serious trout fishers also do their preparation. While it may be subtly different from that which a hunter commits to there are useful parallels. When fishing in a new area it pays to find out as much as possible about it first. While anglers and hunters are both notoriously tight-lipped about where they achieve their best results many involved in both pursuits are quite happy to impart generously with information about general areas and the techniques which are most apt. While a hunter seeking information might enquire at a Department of Conservation office or contact a representative of the local branch of the New Zealand Deerstalkers Association an angler would be well advised to seek advice from Fish and Game New Zealand or local angling clubs. While not all the "trade secrets" will be revealed useful intelligence may be gathered. Good anglers try to ensure that their equipment is well-suited to the particular situation they are attempting to exploit. There is no place for an eight or nine weight rod and line combination on a small West Coast spring creek for example.

Just as hunters venture into magnificent terrain so too do anglers, especially those prepared to get away from main roads. While it is doubtful if there is any water left which has not been explored by at least one adventurous angler these days there are still places which see very few trout fishers. Interestingly some of these are not necessarily the most remote from civilisation, but they do share one common feature, and that is simply that they are difficult to access. The serious angler seeks out these places. Sometimes the most remote places are not the best option. Many a keen back-packing angler has spent days walking into the wilds of Kahurangi National Park, for instance, anticipating solitude as few places in this country are as far from a roadhead, only to have a helicopter disgorge its passengers onto the river bed just minutes after leaving civilisation. While responsible helicopter-borne anglers do everything in their power to avoid scenarios like this there are a few who simply don't care if they ruin someone else's fishing trip. Unfortunately some places have been "discovered" to a degree which we find staggering considering that as little as twenty or so years ago they were rarely visited by anyone.

Hunters and anglers share this love of beautiful places. Indeed, it is one of the main driving forces which motivates us. Les and I have done our time exploring over the years. The search for the "holy grail" took us to many remote, sometimes dangerous places where a mishap may have proved serious. We had many adventures. Great beauty may be found on a stream close to a sizeable centre of population. I've enjoyed fishing the evening rise on the tiny Maitai just minutes from the centre of Nelson, seemingly a million miles from the hustle and bustle of this busy centre. Residents of Napier and Hastings have superb angling right on the doorstep with productive rivers such as the Tuki Tuki and Ngaruoro. Similarly, a duck hunter cocooned in his mai mai alongside a pond on a busy dairy farm can enjoy a remarkable degree of solitude. One place I hunt boasts a vista of startling splendour. The sunset over the range to the west is often spectacular. On many occasions I have watched shadows advance over a high alpine basin, inexorably snuffing out the fiery red/gold tussocks. Sharply etched ridges stretching away seemingly forever belie the existence of towns, roads and people. It is easy to lose oneself in these places. So be it for we fish and hunt partly to experience these things.

A duck hunter checking out a pond or river backwater looks for evidence that waterfowl are using it by searching for tell-tale footprints and especially tiny feathers discarded in the grooming process. A place without clues like these is hardly likely to suddenly become attractive to ducks. Similarly, a deer hunter, seeking an area holding stags during the rutting season looks for signs — hoofprints, recent droppings, wallow holes and shrubs recently rubbed by antlers. He observes places where deer emerge to feed and which ridges they choose to head back to sanctuary on. The prevailing winds are studied and an approach planned accordingly.

The serious trout fisher approaches a water body with caution, just as alert as any hunter to clues which provide an edge. The presence of birds like swallows and terns swooping unerringly on hapless emerging mayflies is always a wonderful sight, promising good sport. I always like to peer into the shallows of any given stream and quietly observe the degree of nymphal activity. It is no accident that the best days I have experienced coincided with much greater than normal insect activity. In mid-summer the cacophony of cicadas tells its own story as does the presence of large numbers of grasshoppers, passion vine hoppers or caddis flies. Sometimes rises may be so subtle as to be almost undetectable, especially on bright, windy days. If little insect activity is obvious it still pays to check under rocks for just what species and size of nymphs are present in the stream. In still waters look for water boatmen, bullies or chironimids. Observation is the key.

What really sets the expert apart from the also-ran hunter or angler is stalking ability. Some have a natural penchant for the business of hunting fish or game and do so almost instinctively. Others need to learn or be actively taught the skills. Some hunters enjoy remarkable success hunting deer in the dense forest lands of New Zealand while many are very rarely ever successful in the bush. It is pertinent to ask just what skills this minority possess which sets them apart. Observational skills have already been alluded to, and this is a major factor in the equation, but others include an ability to concentrate totally for considerable periods of time, the skill to adapt one's approach according to subtle changes in terrain, vegetation types and weather conditions and the confidence to trust one's instincts and senses. I have, at times, hunted with individuals who seem to possess that extra "something" which sets them apart, enabling them to make more contacts with animals than others in the party. It is not chance that they do so.

The ability to concentrate totally is a key component of successful trout stalking. Careless, hurried movements which result in rocks being banged together, bow waves pushed ahead of the angler, showing oneself high above the water and unnatural movement of foliage will all militate against the angler. Bright or highly contrasting clothing will also help to alert ever wary trout.

I have met few anglers with the ability to maintain a high level of concentration for long periods of time. One former client who I will call John was a remarkable exception to this. John is an American who spends a large part of his life travelling throughout Asia in the course of his IT-related job. He works hard, earns a great deal of money and spends it on trips to New Zealand for "the best trout fishing in the world without doubt." When he arrived to fish with me he was always affable, full of one-liners and new jokes — seemingly totally relaxed; that is until he hit the river. Not renowned for making an early start (something I always found very frustrating) we rarely commenced fishing before 10.00am. But when we did all joking ceased. We were into serious stalking mode. Absolutely nothing was left to chance. John is a seriously addicted, self-confessed equipment man. Enormous duffel bags full of every type of angling paraphernalia imaginable accompanied him in the vehicle. On one occasion he even produced a #1 weight rod with matching reel and line and claimed to have caught a respectable trout with it. To me an inordinate amount of time was spent choosing a rod and line combination for the day, rigging up, checking knots over and over and asking question after question. The jokes were discarded. Despite being a giant of a man John was positively sylph-like when it came to sneaking around the river. Never have I observed such total resolve and concentration. Catching trout came into the same realm as achieving success in business, something he had proved himself remarkably adept at. No stone was left unturned in this single-minded pursuit. John was the total angler. A superb caster with an ability to throw a five weight line up into a near gale and with accuracy to boot, he ensured that he would succeed. I never experienced a blank outing with him. At the end of the day, which was always a long one, he would gradually unwind again, and before long the, "Did you hear the one about . . . ?" jokes would start up again. We were always royally entertained around the dinner table with hilarious anecdotes and even more jokes.

I have always believed that something can and should be learned every time one ventures forth to fish for trout. This may sound somewhat insincere, but I believe in this implicitly, for to retain an open mind, receptive to new ideas is how we evolve as anglers. John was one who was always seeking to improve his fishing prowess. He learnt techniques from me and other New Zealand guides, but just as importantly I learned from him. It was he who taught me the "Colorado high stick" technique a method of effectively fishing deep, fast water close to a heavily vegetated or overhanging bank, a simple way of getting nymphs deep and slowing their passage through water which was otherwise almost impossible to fish well.

John was always experimenting with fly tying materials, and there was no limit to his ingenuity. A masterful creator of flies for every imaginable situation, he always came armed with his latest efforts, mostly tied as a means of relaxing in some soulless Asian hotel room on his business trips. The search for new and exotic fly tying materials continues to this day. A tackle store owner's dream come true, he never ceased to amaze me with the new and latest gadget or innovation.

We probably don't need to fish with the intensity of John for we all have our own reasons for fishing and eventually develop our own style. He is though, an example of the angler who so readily embraces the philosophy that to fish well is something which we can influence by choice rather than to leave to chance. I believe that there is a middle path. Try as we might we cannot hope to ever master fly fishing. Striving to improve is laudable, but we must never lose sight of the fact that all forms of recreational fishing are fun, and stalking to catch trout is arguably the most fun of all.

Bibliography

Brooks, Charles E. 1974: *The Trout and The Stream*. Crown.

Bucknall, Geoffrey 1980: Modern Techniques of Still Water Fly-Fishing. Muller.

Clark, Brian 1975: The Pursuit of Still Water Trout. A & C Black.

Elliott, J.M. 1994: Quantitative Ecology and the Brown Trout. Oxford University Press.

Hayes, John W, Stark, John D. and Shearer, Karen A. 2000: Developement and test of a whole-lifetime foraging and bioenergetics growth model for drift feeding brown trout. Transactions of the American Fisheries Society 129: 315-32.

Hayes, J.W. and Jowett, IG 1994: Microhabitat models of large drift-feeding brown trout in three New Zealand rivers. North American Journal of Fisheries Management 14:710-725

Hayes, John W. and Quarterman, Aron J. 2005: Modelling Trout Growth in the Hurunui River. Cawthron Report No. 845 — Prepared for Fish & Game New Zealand.

Hayes, John and Hill, Les 2005: The Artful Science of Trout Fishing. University of Canterbury Press, Christchurch.

Hill, Les 1997: Stalking Stillwaters. Halcyon Press, Auckland

Hill, Les and Marshall, Graeme 1985: Stalking Trout. Halcyon Press, Auckland.

Hill, Les and Marshall, Graeme 1991: Catching Trout. Halcyon Press, Auckland.

Marinaro, Vincent C. 1976: In The Ring of the Rise. Crown.

Marsh, Norman 1983: Trout Stream Insects of New Zealand. Millwood Press.

Merwin, John 1980: Still Water Trout. Nick Lyons Books.

Rosenbauer, Tom 1980: Reading Trout Streams — A Orvis Guide. Nick Lyons Books.

Skues, G.E.M. 1921: The Way of a Trout with a Fly. A & C Black.

Sosin, Mark and Clark, John 1976: Through the Fish's Eye. Andre Deutsch.

Watson, Rupert 1993: The Trout. Swan-Hill Press.